W9-BTH-983

MOVING MINUS MISHAPS

A Practical Guide for Successful Family Relocation Including Foreign and Domestic Moves

by Beverly D. Roman

MICHAEL CADIEUX 90

 BR Anchor Publishing, Bethlehem, Pennsylvania

This publication is designed to provide accurate and authoritative information in regard to the subject matter covered. In publishing this book, neither the author nor the publisher is engaged in rendering legal, accounting or other professional service. If legal advice or other expert assistance is required, the services of a competent professional should be sought.

Printed in the United States of America
© 1991, BR Anchor Publishing
P.O. Box 176, Hellertown, PA 18055-0176
All Rights Reserved
ISBN 9627470-0-9
Library of Congress Number 90-083538
Edited by Paula J. Brisco

Nancy J. Adler, *International Dimensions of Organizational Behavior*, 2nd ed. (Boston: PWS-Kent Publishing Company, 1991), p.229,274. PWS-Kent Publishing Company is a division of Wadsworth, Incorporated. Reprinted with permission of PWS-Kent Publishing Company

Mover's Advantage, Ryder Truck Rental, Incorporated. Reprinted with permission of Ryder System, Incorporated

"Real Estate Briefs," *RE/MAX Times*, Vol.9, Number 6. Published for Mary Omdahl, with RE/MAX 100 Real Estate, by Personal Marketing Company, a RE/MAX International Incorporated supplier. Reprinted with permission of Personal Marketing Company

"Get a house without spending a lot of cash," by Joe Kilsheimer of *The Orlando Sentinel* printed in *The Morning Call*, November 5, 1989. Copyright November 5, 1989. Reprinted with permission of *The Morning Call*

*This book is dedicated to all my family,
especially to those who prevailed through our
many moving adventures.*

ACKNOWLEDGMENTS

Thank you to my family—namely Stan, Amy, Rick and Chris—who graciously responded when asked to read this sentence, paragraph, page, "just one more time" and for their help, encouragement and patience throughout the writing of this book. Thank you also to my sister Judy Cadieux, her husband, Dr. Roger J. Cadieux, Everett and Wilma Mills, Joan Hyland, Richard Waterbury, John Roach, James O. Boyce, Pat Schantz, and Mary Omdahl who kindly offered their time and their comments.

CONTENTS

PART I
Practical Information to Organize a Move

PART II

*International Relocation and
Additional Topics*

CHECKLISTS

The following checklists are in the back of the book. These are
also incorporated in various chapters and reference to them will
be "boxed" and "starred." There are blank pages for notes following the checklists.

Introduction

My husband I have been married for 29 years and in that time we made a total of 16 moves. These moves were usually not by choice, but rather a result of naval assignment changes or corporate career moves.

My sister-in-law, Barbara, told me many times, "You should write a book." My reply was always the same, "Yes, but no one would believe it!" However, the mishaps and funny things that happened (some funny only in retrospect) did serve as learning tools for subsequent moves. My husband and I also learned how to expedite the fundamentals that are necessary for every move.

During our fifteenth move, which was a return to the United States after a three and one-half year assignment in England, I decided to share some relocation tips and hints to others facing the overwhelming task of a move, whether across the state or across the ocean. These hints will especially help those I consider the real "heroes" in the moving process—the partners who remain behind to orchestrate the move after the transferee has left to begin a new position.

The purpose of this book is to help you make your move as positive an experience as possible. It will give you guidelines for a smooth move from one home to another. As I write these words, I know there is no such thing as a smooth move, but perhaps the book will even up the odds a bit and give you a fighting chance!

As the contents indicate, this book is outlined in two parts. Part I will give you the practical and necessary chapters to organize a move, primarily in the United States. Part II covers international relocation and offers other practical topics for your consideration.

One of the very first movers was an Eskimo.
He wanted to move from his little efficiency igloo
to a more spacious igloo with a view of the Arctic.
All he had to move were three large blocks of ice.
The movers lost one, cracked one
and sent one to Florida.

PART I

PRACTICAL INFORMATION TO ORGANIZE A MOVE

Phone call Tuesday, any Tuesday,
at about ten o'clock
*"Sweetheart, would you like to go out to
dinner this evening?"*

1

"WE ARE MOVING!"

Breaking the News to Your Family

Finding out that a move is on the horizon comes in various ways. I gradually learned that I was about to be presented with a new challenge when I was asked out to dinner on a Tuesday evening—*especially* in the days when my husband and I did not go out to dinner very often.

No matter what the proposed job advancement, I believe most people would rather stay in their comfortable environment than go through the disruption of a move. Moving was never my favorite pastime and I did not jump for joy at the thought. However, whenever the possibility of a relocation presented itself, my husband and I discussed it and how it would affect our family. If we decided to relocate, we proceeded to tell our children, presenting as many details as seemed appropriate for their ages.

Children do not want to have the world as they know it disturbed any more than parents do. Protests will surely be heard. Predictably, the present school (which was never as good as the former school) takes on a note of excellence. Friends who were questionable will now be viewed as bosom buddies. How this situation is handled will be a key factor in the way the upcoming move is perceived. It is most important for the entire family to believe the relocation is the right choice.

Work Force in the Nineties

The nineties have brought about an entirely new work force!

1

Twenty-eight years ago, it was traditional for the husband to be the breadwinner in the family and the wife to organize most everything for the children and the home, which meant basically anything with an unknown job description. Moving fell into this category. Today, the dual-career marriage is more typical and it becomes a choice of whose career path to follow.

Moves may be greeted enthusiastically by the individual who is offered a job opportunity but apprehensively by the spouse who does not want to relocate. With dual-career marriages on the upswing (at least 56 percent in 1987, according to government statistics), spouses may have excellent positions in their own right. The geographic area of the new job may not offer the opportunity for the spouse to earn his or her present salary or hold a similar job position.

Relocating a family is never easy. It involves finding a new dwelling, new doctors, new schools, new music teachers or, more simply, a "new everything." Moving may be one of the most taxing challenges you ever face as a couple and as a family. Some experts think a move falls in the same emotional category as finding a new job or getting a divorce. It is a culture shock no matter what the circumstance—moving a state away, across America or to another country. It's therefore imperative to keep the situation in perspective and to support each other. Therein lies one of the many challenges. As my husband reasons, "We don't have problems, we have challenges." Some days they may seem like problems, so you have to keep repeating that sentence. *Some days you may have to repeat it a lot!*

Relocating our family as many times as we did (a dubious honor) meant that some stays had to be relatively short. Our shortest stay was in California.

> *We moved into our California home on October 2, sold it on November 5, and moved out on December 27 (to Pittsburgh, Pennsylvania)!*

We later, *much later*, joked that we were probably the only people to buy a home for our family vacation. Can you imagine the challenge to our children of going to three schools in one year, not to mention the challenge of tax preparation for

2

three states in the same year?

Multiple residences make it difficult for young people to say where their hometown is, especially when they arrive in college. When our son Rick started at the University of Notre Dame, the personal stories he related to his friends contained such a variety of cities and states that many students wondered just which town was actually his home.

Moving presents a myriad of changes, so you should give considerable thought to whether this move is worthwhile for all concerned. When you make the decision to move, *support* is the key word for everyone. This cannot be emphasized enough. With so many changes taking place and with so many new demands on your time, you can easily overlook that family member who is having an extremely difficult time with the upcoming move and all it entails. Sometimes the fear of losing friends, of losing a position on sports teams or cheerleading squad, or any one of a hundred things can cause anxious moments for your child. As we were preparing our house and ourselves for a departure from one city, our second

grader looked into the refrigerator one day and asked, "Are we getting poor?" As I realized that he associated the empty refrigerator with possible poverty, I carefully explained to him how close we were to the departure date and why we were depleting our supplies.

No move is a breeze. Though one may proceed more smoothly than another, none is easy or fun. I compare it to having a baby—just as you are going through the delivery (especially at the end), you might say, "I will *never* do this again." However, time has a way of diminishing memory of the discomfort. When you look in on the little darling at night (always at night and when the child is fast asleep), you say to yourself, "Gosh that wasn't so bad." So it is with a move. Eventually you do forget the mishaps and possibly you will even get all your boxes emptied before the next move—or before your children get married, whichever comes first.

Figures released in September 1990 by the U.S. Census Bureau Poplulation Division indicated that 43,693,000 people, or 18.6 percent of our population, relocated in 1986/1987 (the last year for which figures were available.) This number includes people moving within the United States and to the United States from another country. The majority of these people relocate with little or no guidance in planning their move. How you approach the move and the upcoming new situation is going to set the tone for the way your whole family will accept it. This is definitely your most difficult role in this unfolding drama.

2

GETTING STARTED

The greatest number of people who relocate do so between May and October. If you are planning a move during this time, you should reserve dates and equipment as soon as possible. This applies to moving with professional movers or moving on your own with rental equipment.

As soon as you know you are moving contact several moving companies and compare cost estimates, pick-up and delivery procedures, insurance protection plan and services (for instance some companies will move houseplants if the distance is not too great). Allow an extra day or two beyond your scheduled departure date for unforseen complications or delays.

Next contact the newspaper in your new location and have some Sunday editions mailed to you. A newspaper will help you become familiar with the area's real estate market, mortgage rates, news, theaters, places of interest and school activities and sporting events.

Lists (and Lists and More Lists)

Begin early and make daily lists of anything that is relevant to your family situation. Some suggestions are:

1. **Compose a list for address changes.** Obtain change-of-address-forms from your local post office and inform the postmaster of the new address and date as soon as you know it. Consider placing these on your address-change list:

- car registration
- driver's license
- voter registration
- college bursar's office
- insurances
- bank

5

- magazines
- investments

- credit cards
- frequent flier club

The address-change list you compile should be saved so that you can keep using it, deleting or adding as necessary. It will make the next move easier, because you will always have a list of addresses that will need to be changed.

2. **Contact service and utility companies.** Contact the business offices for remaining bills and leave a forwarding address for billing. Some suggestions:

- newspaper
- gas company
- dry cleaner
- oil service
- television and cable
- lawn care service

- trash collector
- electric company
- local telephone
- long-distance telephone
- diaper service

3. **Itemize the necessities to take with you.** As you proceed through your day, write down anything that you may need before your household goods arrive at your new location, or that you may have a difficult time being without as you move into your new home. Having all your belongings delivered to your new home does not guarantee that you can *find anything* with relative ease. Make sure you include all necessary medications for your family. If you are driving to your new location, and have the room, a small supply of cooking utensils is handy, as well as a kettle for boiling water. Take along your old telephone directory—it will be good for referral for doctors, dentists, pharmacists, businesses previously used, and addresses and telephone numbers of friends.

In addition to these lists, I have outlined other areas that are well worth considering during a move. They were developed for our own convenience and as a result of experiences we would not like repeated.

---

* Note: There are more detailed checklists for each list in the back of the book.

Household Inventory

Make a household inventory! This is something you should

6

have whether you move or not. It is to your advantage to compile a detailed, room-by-room inventory, making notes on current replacement values for all your household goods as you go along. The inventory should be updated regularly for many reasons, but especially for insurance purposes. Furniture or possessions that are particularly valuable should be documented with photographs. There are items in your home and your jewelry box that you do not use daily and that you might not miss for months after you move into your home. If you discover an item missing, it is very helpful to have it described and documented in an inventory and with your insurance company. We experienced a loss during one move and, as a result, could not replace a treasured family piece.

File for Pertinent Records

Recommendations for this file are:
- medical and dental insurance forms
- insurance identification card with group number
- insurance forms or some identification of insurance number for your auto
- pertinent medical records
- dental records
- children's inoculation records, if necessary for school
- school records and birth certificates (in case children start school before your household goods arrive)
- names of readers or materials children are using in school
- registration forms
- necessary legal forms and contracts for your home purchase
- prescriptions for medications and eyeglasses

THE MOVE IS IN TWO DAYS, WHAT ARE YOU SO WORRIED ABOUT ?

7

- bankbook and/or statement
- map of your new city

* Note the checklist for file in the back of the book.

Any records that can be duplicated or copied should be. If you cannot duplicate this material, put it where *no one* will disturb it. During our move from England to America I prepared a file for all our important papers, which was rather a complicated process due to our international status. Somehow this file disappeared one day. It has yet to be found! The time of this loss was a particularly busy period for us due to the move and having several houseguests simultaneously. Rebuilding this lost file became another (very large) challenge. After I finally reassembled most of the information, I vowed to tape the next file to my body.

Telephone Contacts

Remember to give family members and close friends the telephone number and address of your temporary living quarters. If the information is not immediately available, give friends and family the name of someone or someplace to contact in case of emergency. This could be your motel, your new office or a future neighbor. When you acquire a new telephone number, the information operator will not have that listing for at least two to four days after telephone installation. Be sure to carry the telephone numbers of your family members with you.

Again, the best way to determine what is necessary for your lists or files is to make notes of anything that you believe you should not be without, whether for convenience, safety or legal reasons. And remember to begin compiling lists early, perhaps months ahead of your targeted moving date.

Survival Boxes

Start a moving-day survival box and include the following items:

- paper, pen, pencil, marking pen and stamps
- cellophane tape and heavy-duty tape

- scissors
- tape measure
- paper cups (hot and cold), paper plates, disposable utensils
- instant coffee, tea, sugar and powdered creamer
- storage bags with a zipper closure
- paper towels, soap, disposable towelettes and toilet tissue
- adhesive bandages and aspirin
- travel alarm
- small tool kit and a flashlight
- can opener/bottle opener/corkscrew
- a gallon of bottled drinking water
- litter bag or container for your trip

Include anything else that you consider necessary to your particular situation. House keys for the new home, if you have them. Spare car keys to your car. Set aside an ice chest for use on moving day for cold beverages or items that require refrigeration.

Place the survival box somewhere where it will be undisturbed and untapped by family members so that during moving week you have it all in hand. You can make up boxes for different situations and different people.

> * Note the checklist for the survival box in the back of the book.

Children's Survival Boxes

Making a survival box is a good job for children, as long as you believe they are old enough to handle the situation. If your youngsters can write, they can make a list of anything they will need in the new home before the household goods arrive. This could include some of their treasures to make them feel at home.

A word of caution: Give the children a small box for this purpose, since it is meant to be for the trip. A small box will limit the size of the objects they will pack. When we began using the survival box idea, we had a difficult time dissuading our three-year-old son Chris from packing his entire collection of stuffed animals as we prepared to depart from California (by plane of course). He considered them all necessary, and to him, they were.

For other chores, engage anyone who can write or print. There is always something children can do, such as make lists for you or for themselves, sort through their outgrown toys or move light items from room to room. Anything that will help in your organization before the move will eventually expedite the procedure when you arrive at your destination. By involving the children, you help create excitement for and anticipation of their new environment.

3

SELLING A HOME

Tips to Obtain the Best Price for Your Home

Fix your home as attractively as possible. Buyers see *at least* 12 to 20 homes before they make an offer and ultimately purchase a home. Some real estate agents believe the buyer makes a decision during the first 20 minutes of seeing a home. First-time impressions, therefore, are extremely important. Or, as my grandmother used to say, "You never get a second chance to make a first impression."

"Curb appeal" is a critical factor. When you view this home from the street, do you want to venture inside? Are the trees, the shrubs and the lawn well-manicured? Is there debris around the property? Are the paint, windows, shutters, mailbox, front door in good condition? Stand away from the home and walk around the outside to view it critically as though seeing through someone else's eyes. Depending on the season of the year, you can add some colorful plants to enhance the property.

Set your price realistically. Pricing is important. You do not want to turn people away by demanding an outrageous price and you do not want to lose money on the sale. Know what similar homes have been selling for. Compare the quality, size (including the number of rooms), renovations and condition of your home to others that have sold in the neighborhood, and consider these features when setting your price. Check with a real estate agent on a suggested price, and place your house on the market as soon as you know your projected moving plans.

Initial impression. The first thing one should notice upon entering a home is a nice clean fragrance. To create a welcoming fragrance, you can either simmer a few cloves or a lemon slice in water or place a little vanilla on a warm light bulb. If these hints are not practical, you should at least make sure there are no offensive odors such as animal odors in your home.

Avoid clutter. The home should be as orderly and clean as possible. Some suggestions: Remove excess appliances from the countertop. Place fresh towels in the bathroom. Organize the closets. Put children's toys in a container or place them somewhere neatly. Windows, drapes, curtains and shades should be clean and without tears or breakage.

Neutral colors. If you have very unusual colors in the paint or paper, consider changing to a more neutral color. If you change the paint, use light colors to give a room a larger appearance.

Realtor and buyer privacy. Give real estate agents and potential buyers some time to themselves to discuss the home and let the agents do their job. Be available for questions, if necessary, but try to stay in the background. Inform your agent of the annual maintenance and utility costs of your home. Have available the necessary literature and warranties for whatever appliances are to be sold with the house.

Last walk-through. Walk through your home just before the real estate agent arrives to check for any last minute details. Remember, the first impression the buyer has upon entering your home may make the decision for the sale.

Termination of services after the sale. Make arrangements to terminate all utilities, insurance and services that you have on your home. The date should be the same as the settlement date. Request that a "payoff statement" from the institution holding your mortgage be sent to your lawyer. All liabilities for which you are responsible should be paid by the settlement date. A forwarding address should be given for the remaining statements. Do not pay taxes due after the closing on the house. The new owners will make their own arrangements for the services to begin in the home.

Settlement day—the day when the buyer and seller transfer ownership of the house, often referred to as the closing on the house. You should consider having a lawyer for settlement, particularly if you are not knowledgeable about home buying and selling procedures, to ensure you have the necessary papers for your settlement. If you do not know a lawyer, check with a reliable business associate or the "Lawyer Referral Service" in the Yellow Pages of your telephone directory. Obtain all your closing costs to review *before the settlement date.*

For valuable free information, look in the Yellow Pages of your telephone directory under "Real Estate." Some real estate firms specify relocation in their advertisements. Many of these offices have free booklets that provide advice on buying or selling a home, including advice on tax benefits, home financing and helpful hints on home maintenance.

Real estate agents can outline for you the costs and taxes involved in selling a home. Note the tax details in Chapter 22, Tax Structure—Home Sales, written by a certified public accountant.

---

* Note the checklist for selling a home in the back of the book.

"Oh, is it really 7:30?
I left my watch at home
and we had no idea of the time."

4

PLANNING A GARAGE SALE

A garage sale is a good way to clear your present home of unwanted articles before they are packed and moved to the new home. The motto is "One person's junk is someone else's treasure." Just don't sell the garage!

The garage sale I had in England confused some people because the British people call this sale a boot sale or rubbish sale. Some of my British friends came to my garage sale to watch the fun of *selling the garage!*

Timing. Begin by picking a convenient weekend, preferably one when you will have some help, as the endeavor requires several people to manage it well. It is advisable to conduct a sale with a friend or several friends. Multiple family sales are a super way to share the work and the newspaper advertisement costs. Multiple sales also provide a greater variety of goods and turn out to be a lot more fun.

After you have picked your days (Fridays and Saturdays are good), go through your home room by room, closet by closet, deciding what you may never need again. If you have moved often and have an item you have unpacked four or more times and have not used, it deserves to go to a new owner. Check with your children for outgrown toys, games, books or puzzles.

Salable items. Jewelry, furniture, lamps, tools, small (and large) appliances, books, records, games, puzzles, toys and sports equipment usually sell well. Basically, mark and display anything that you cannot use. The item may sell. Clothing in general does not move quickly, with the exception of jeans, jackets, scarves, belts, and unusual apparel such as college sweatshirts or team shirts. Mark each item with size to encourage interest.

Houseplants. Plants add color to your sale and are popular purchases. If you have a large number of plant containers to sell, buy an economical flat of flowering plants and put one plant in each container. This will make the container more attractive to a customer. If you are moving a long distance or flying to your next destination, you can sell all your houseplants.

Marking system. We have found the color-code method successful. Purchase packs of different colored dots (the kind with a self-adhesive) at a local variety store and make a color chart. One color represents one dollar, another 50 cents, and so on. Place the appropriate color sticker on your items. You can use blank stickers for other prices. This whole marking procedure is much easier than you might think. Save plastic and brown bags from stores for customers to use for their (large) purchases.

Pricing items. You must "think garage sale." You cannot always gauge the price you place on an item by the actual dollar value it would command in a store. The price on this item depends on the condition, the current popularity (it may be hopelessly out of style) and its age. If you have never had a sale, you can peruse other people's sales before you have your own. This will give you hints on pricing.

By the second day of your sale, you must decide if you want to keep any of your remaining items. If not, lower the price. During the last hour of the sale, make a loud announcement: "All things left will go at half the listed price."

Remember, for some people garage-sale shopping is a way of life. For some, it even is their life. These people will try to pay a minimum price for your goods no matter what the value. When you tell them this item is a priceless family heirloom and you are parting with it *solely* for lack of space (that and you need the money for college tuition), their reply will be to offer you 50 cents instead of 10 cents for the item.

Change for the sale. Have change for the dollar available for your customers. Wear an old apron with pockets if you have one, or some article of clothing with several pockets.

Advertisement. If you have a multifamily sale, a large advertisement highlighting unique items, such as furniture, golf clubs, trains or anything unusual, will definitely be a plus. Mention the dates and times and give brief directions for your sale. Advertise on both days of the sale. The extent to which you advertise depends on the size of your sale and how many people are sharing the costs. If you are paying for the ad yourself, then you have to decide whether the amount of goods you have will warrant the extra expense. Take advantage of any free advertisement that is available, such as bulletin boards in grocery stores and dry-cleaning establishments. Post signs at busy intersections and significant areas near your home on the days of the sale to direct people to your home. This will also attract motorists who have not seen the advertisement in the newspaper or stores.

On the first morning of the sale, keep the garage door down until you are ready to begin. People have a way of arriving early, such as 7:30 a.m. instead of the announced starting time of 9:00 a.m. These early birds are "regulars," and they pretend to be unaware of the time in order to look over the goods before the crowds arrive.

Leftover items. Charitable organizations are usually willing to pick up whatever they think they can use or sell. It should make you smile to think that there will be less to unpack at your next house, and you will be a bit wealthier for the effort.

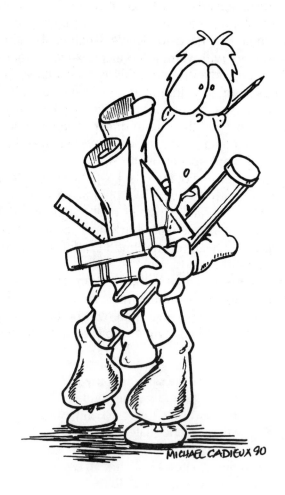

5

BUY, BUILD OR RENT A HOME

The values you put on whether to buy, build or rent depend to some extent on how long you will be in a particular area. Do you have enough money for a down payment on a home? If you cannot afford a down payment, note the suggestions in Chapter 9, Real Estate Agents and Mortgages in the section by Joe Kilsheimer on buying without a down payment. Is this a long-term or a short-term investment? If you have sold a home, it is usually more prudent to buy a home unless you are moving to a foreign country, and then it will depend on the tax structure of that particular country and your own circumstances.

Buying a Home

One of the fondest dreams of most people is to own their own house. This is by far one of the largest investments many of us make in a lifetime, taking on many thousands of dollars of debt. Despite the enormity of this undertaking, many of us approach home buying without having done enough research. Often we are inadequately informed.

Buying a dwelling (home, townhouse or condominium) is generally considered a good investment, especially when you consider renting as an alternative. Rental money is never seen after you send it to the landlord. When you purchase a home, your monthly payments are working for you, and you will gain tax compensations as well. Your monthly house payments will be stable (if you have a fixed mortgage), unlike rents, which can and do escalate.

Today buying a home is no longer considered primarily a

family endeavor. Adults are remaining single longer, starting families later, and purchasing homes on their own more than ever before. The Federal Housing Administration and government bond programs offer loans with lower interest rates and, as a result, houses have become more accessible to the single person.

Additional information on this subject can be found in Chapter 22, Tax Structure—Home Sales and in the section of Chapter 21 addressing local real estate taxes, zoning and property transfer taxes.

Buying an Older Home

For many people there is a certain charm in an older home. Older homes display architectural features and possess living areas that one generally does not find in newer, more modern structures. Many old buildings contain deep windowsills, large hallways, large porches, high ceilings, quaint fixtures and many of the nostalgic appointments that we perhaps loved as children or have seen in magazines or movies.

At times people buy old homes because the price is right. If you are handy with tools and have the time, you can fix up an old home very reasonably. If these homes have been on the market for a considerable length of time, they may be even more of a bargain. However, there can be problems. You could end up with the proverbial "money pit" if you are not careful.

Engage a *professional building inspector* and have this person carefully check the house for problems. On occasion, the inspector may suggest other professionals to look at the house. This is money well spent if you do not know the signs and symptoms of potential house problems.

The building's structure should be scrutinized along with the heating and plumbing systems, roof, windows, electrical system and drains. Know if the home warrants radon testing. Check the foundation and basement walls for cracking. Fireplaces should be carefully checked for residue buildup inside the chimney. With an older home you have to expect more routine maintenance and fewer of the easy-to-maintain surfaces and appliances found in newer homes.

Consider whether you like some of the modern conveniences that are available today for homes. For instance, if you would like to have a whirlpool bath or a sauna in your home in the future, would the older home lend itself to renovation for these features? Can the electrical wiring accommodate electronic additions or air-conditioning if that is not already in the house? Estimated costs of repairs and improvements should be added to the "bargain price" for the older home.

Building as an Option

Building is an option if you cannot find a house that will fit your needs or is located in one of the areas you desire to live. If your position is transient or temporary, building may not be a wise option. Building requires more time initially; therefore, you will need short-term living quarters during this phase and then have another move after the house is completed. Some or all household items can be stored, depending on your short-term rental situation. Allow enough time for building *and delays* when you sign your rental agreement.

Many people think they get more house for their money by building. Also, building can provide you with a home tailored

to your individual family's needs and requirements. Depending on your relocation timing, the style or size home you desire to purchase may not be available. Building is so involved that I have devoted a separate chapter to this subject.

Renting a Dwelling

Sometimes renting a place to live may be your only choice. Pat Schantz from Patt-White Realty Company in Allentown, Pennsylvania, outlined some typical reasons why people rent a home, apartment, townhouse or condominium:

1. renting temporarily to see if you like your new position
2. waiting to see if you like a new area
3. waiting to find a house in an area in which you desire to reside
4. being in a position for a short period before moving to another city
5. waiting for a house to be built
6. unable to have your expenses assumed by your company for buying and selling a home

Relocation with rental agreements can be difficult. *Be sure to read the lease thoroughly, especially the fine print.* If you need to break a lease for a relocation, or any other reason, you should know what you are responsible for financially. A clause in the lease may permit you to sublease a dwelling, but you could be responsible for damages the alternate tenant incurs. Leases vary for many reasons, and some of these are the owner's circumstances, the type of dwelling, the location of the dwelling, the availability of new tenants, the housing market and possibly the season of the year.

If you are renting a dwelling on a temporary basis, and will not have all your belongings with you, consider taking along some family pictures and a few personal items to make you feel at home in the interim. It is surprising how a few of your favorite things will help ease you through a change in environment.

6

FURNITURE MEASURING TO SCALE

Measuring your furniture is an extremely useful and practical tool for a move. I suggest that anyone looking for a house perform this exercise before beginning the house search. These measurements will provide a more realistic idea of the space required for your furniture. Even though this may sound like a lot of unnecessary work, I promise you it is well worth the effort.

Begin by gathering a yardstick, a tape measure, a pad of paper, a pencil and one assistant. Allow approximately one hour of your time, and proceed to measure all your furniture room by room. Write down the name of the room, the piece of furniture and the furniture's measurements. This endeavor will proceed surprisingly quickly if you use the same order in each room—such as measuring height first, width second, and depth third. Inform your assistant what that order will be and just fly on through.

Drawing Furniture to Scale

The next step takes place preferably when all little children are tucked into bed for the night. Use some type of sturdy paper or three- by five-inch cards and draw small squares or rectangles to resemble each piece of furniture. Use a scale of one-quarter inch equals one foot for the width and depth, writing height on the paper piece in case you need to refer to it later. Identify the pieces, such as "Tom's desk" or "Sally's dresser." Cut these squares out and place them in envelopes labeled appropriately, such as "family room," "living room" or "Tom's room."

These miniature pieces of furniture never get thrown away until *the furniture itself is discarded*. The furniture may get moved from room to room, envelope to envelope, but never thrown away. The paper furniture pieces will be helpful for the new home and invaluable if you are building. We recently built a home, and we actually planned our rooms around most of our furniture.

Unusually Large Pieces of Furniture

Unusually large pieces of furniture, such as a baby grand piano, may require an extra step in this process. In addition to drawing the piece of furniture to scale for your room plot, you can cut a pattern from an old bedsheet for it. Lay the sheet on the furniture and cut around the edge to give you the pattern. You can easily carry the cutout sheet with you as you do your house shopping and lay the fabric on the floor of any home you are considering. In this way you will have a visual conception of the space the piece will consume.

Template

For a small fee (approximately $4 to $10) you can purchase a template at a stationery store. A template resembles a stencil, showing typical household furniture in cutout form. This may not include all your furniture, but you can add pieces as necessary.

Room Plots

Purchase some graph paper and draw your rooms to size. This idea is given with the new home in mind; however, you can use it anytime you want to rearrange your furniture. Measure your rooms and draw them on graph paper, allowing each square to equal one foot. As you make the room plot, note the placement of the windows and doors.

Next you can place the paper furniture pieces on the paper room plot, moving the pieces in various ways to maximize the space available. When you have a satisfactory furniture arrangement, you can draw the furniture squares on the graph paper. Make one plot for each room.

Save these room plots, just as you did the furniture pieces. It is extremely helpful to post these in the rooms of your new home on moving day. The plots can also be used later to rearrange a room. This saves time and *lots* of energy!

"IS THIS JUST NOT PERFECT HONEY!"

7

HOME SHOPPING

Finding the Perfect Home

Finding the perfect home is like finding the perfect mate. There is no such phenomenon. There are many things essential to a good marriage; however, one of the blessings that will carry you far is to find someone who has faults with which you can live. It is much the same thing with a home. There is no perfect home, but if you can find one that has faults you can live with, repair or remodel, then that is a home in which you can be reasonably comfortable. (By "home" the author means a dwelling, whether it is a house, a condominium or a townhouse.)

Define Your Goals

Your first goal is to define in your own mind exactly what you want in a home and what your needs are as a family. The rooms that you consider necessary, or that you particularly liked in your last home, should be well thought out. No feature is too obvious or too trivial; include them all. Talk this over with the whole family, making a list of your needs and wants. The "needs" list will narrow your search by eliminating those houses that are hopelessly wrong for you. Your "wants" list will help you choose between the possibilities. What are your future needs? Is your family growing? Getting smaller? Will you be starting a business and possibly need an office in your home? Each family must decide what is best for its situation, present and future.

27

Selecting an Area

Initially you should allot ample time to survey the area with one or two real estate agents. Allow time in your schedule for mortgage shopping and school shopping. Anticipate that you may need several trips to your new location to adequately address these concerns. Note whether there are possible playmates or a playground in the area for your children. Conveniently located school bus stops are a consideration, especially if your children are very young.

Some questions to ask yourself while making your decision are: What type of transportation is available? Do we need a second car in this new location? (When my husband and I had to learn to drive on the "other" side of the road in England, we were not at all sure we even wanted a car.) What are the functions and activities that take place in our daily life? How far will we have to travel to work? school? church? airport? doctor? hospital? grocery store? Little League? Can the children cycle to functions safely? Is there a day-care center nearby?

The next thing to consider is whether you are a country person or a city person. What atmosphere and activities does your family enjoy? Research each community that you think will fit your needs. Is this an area that will appreciate in value? Have you met any of the neighbors? What is the atmosphere in the neighborhood, and do you feel comfortable with the people you meet? Ask the people if they enjoy living in the neighborhood. Go through the neighborhood at different times of the day. Ride by school bus stops to get a feel for the children in the area. Are the lawns and homes neat and well kept?

Environmental Issues

It is well worth your time to investigate the environmental issues that affect an area you are considering. Know, for instance, if the homes warrant radon testing. Your real estate agent will most likely be aware of the ways to check into these issues. The library and the local newspaper should be able to help you find sources of environmental information, along with addresses and names of contacts.

Additional information can be found in the section of Chapter 21, addressing local real estate taxes, zoning, and property transfer taxes, outlined by an attorney.

Pictures and the Floor Plan

If you find a house that you really like and are now making a commitment on this house, request permission to measure the rooms and take any pictures that will be helpful. The room measurements are crucial, and again this does not take long with an assistant. Be sure to note the size and placement of windows and doors.

Pictures serve a dual purpose. They refresh your memory after seeing so many houses and are nice to show to family members who cannot get to see the house beforehand. You can show them pictures and discuss how you will decorate the rooms, especially their own, to suit their taste. This will help your children get prepared for and possibly even excited about their new home.

When you have your floor plan, you can draw your rooms to scale on graph paper, penciling in the doors and windows. The details of measuring furniture are outlined in Chapter 6, Furniture—Measuring to Scale. Next take the scaled drawings of Sally's furniture or Tom's furniture and begin placing them on the graph paper within the appropriate rooms. Move them around until you key in on the arrangement that makes the best use of each room.

You can now draw the furniture on the room plots for your new home. On moving day post these on the walls of the individual rooms in the new home. The movers will love it! This saves a lot of confusion on the "big day," especially when the movers come through the front door with a heavy sofa and say "Where do you want this piece, lady?" You smile confidently and tell them *exactly* where it should be placed.

The additional sources for selling a home that I mentioned in Chapter 3 will also be helpful for home shopping. Look in the Yellow Pages of your telephone directory for listings that specify relocation in their advertisements. Many of these offices have free booklets available with advice on buying or selling a home including advice on tax benefits, home financing, and numerous other helpful hints on home maintenance.

Real estate agents can outline for you the costs and taxes involved in buying a home. Note the tax details in Chapter 22, Tax Structure—Home Sales written by a certified public accountant. See also: "Noteworthy Additions for Investment and or Resale" and "Improvements—Poor Return on Investments," Chapter 8, Building a Home.

* Note the checklist for home shopping in the back of the book.

NO, NO, I THINK IT LOOKED BETTER OVER BY THAT WINDOW THE FIRST TIME!

8

BUILDING A HOME

Selecting a Builder

If you have decided to build a home, meet with at least three builders to find out all you can about them. It is critical to lay the "personal foundation" before they pour the concrete. You want to feel comfortable with your builder, for you will be working closely with this person for a minimum of nine to 10 months. Inquire about the contractor's techniques, specifications on houses, prices, reputation in the community and financial situation. It's smart to do a credit check on your prospective builder. Check with clients who have used these builders and determine if they are satisfied in all regards. This is the best reference.

Follow-up care after you are firmly entrenched in the home is very important. When meeting with prospective builders, find out what they will do for problems that arise after you are in the home, and obtain something in writing to confirm this fact. Find out which builders finish their houses close to the promised date. Even if a builder has a good reputation for doing so, you should allow an extra four to six weeks for building your home. Serious delays can be caused by all sorts of things that may not be under anyone's control, such as a shortage of materials, inclement weather, damaged products and similar problems.

Timetable for Interior and Exterior Color Choices

Obtain a *projected schedule* from your builder so you are

aware of the timing for choices that must be made, such as the roof and siding color, plumbing and cabinet hardware, tile or vinyl flooring, cabinets and electrical fixtures. Knowing a schedule will help curb last-minute decisions and let you consider your choices for a little while. There are so many choices to be made! A timetable may seem like a minor point; however, as you enter into this project, there are so many things to do and items to select that I cannot emphasize this timetable enough. Important decisions should not be made in haste. Work out a checkoff list with your builder and follow it closely. This ensures that your selections are made when you need them, and it ensures that the builder is adhering to the schedule too.

Early decisions on colors and materials help guarantee availability of the products. It can be very inconvenient, to say the least, to find that you should have ordered something weeks ago, and now you discover the item is on back order or out of stock.

Fine-tuning the Building Plan

Now is the time to get out the cutout paper furniture again. Place the paper pieces on your blueprint to see if it meets your needs. Moving walls or doors on paper before laying the foundation is not that difficult. As you lay furniture pieces on your house plan design, you can tell if a room will be large enough to accommodate the furniture you wish to place there. For instance, as my husband and I laid out the miniature paper furniture on our recent house plan, we realized that the dining room size would be inadequate for the furniture that we had. We then changed the house plan while it was still in the blueprint stage.

If you have a room in your prospective home that you have never had before, measure out an imaginary space the size of the new area using markers such as yardsticks. Will the area fit your needs? Your furniture plan? Draw new rooms on graph paper and place whatever paper furniture you are considering in these rooms. If you will have three feet of walking space between furniture, measure it with markers and walk through the space several times to get a feel for it.

As you finalize the plan, obtain a list of the subcontractors (including telephone numbers and addresses) with whom you will be working. Plumbers, electricians, carpenters, carpet installers, cabinetmakers and tile installers are among the commonly used subcontractors. The names from your builder are only suggestions. If you have the time, I strongly advise comparing prices, quality and performance with other distributers of the same products. Try to see some homes where their work is evident. Inform the subcontractors that you are comparison shopping.

As you get close to a decision on the style of home you are to build, spend as much time as you can going over the plan for sizing, comfort, accessibility, basement entry, mudroom or garret. Examine the plan with a friend, or several friends, who can help guard against overlooking a minor, or major, detail.

Multipurpose Rooms

Building at the age of 48 as opposed to age 28 can make a difference in the size and style of home that you build. Consider making your spare rooms multipurpose rooms. If you have several grown children in your family who come home a few times a year, a large office or den with a sleep sofa would be more practical than a bedroom that would be empty most of the time. There are many other reasons why you could double the use of a spare room into a sewing room, sunny reading room, extra TV room or hobby room. This is a way to cut down on the size of the house, if you so desire, and still have the rooms that you would find useful.

Electrical Outlets—Placement

Displaying your furniture in the projected rooms on paper will help establish areas that require electrical outlets. I think this selection is one of the most difficult aspects of building. At the point in time that you go through the house with the electrician, there are only two-by-fours to resemble the walls where rooms will be. The floor plan with your furniture drawn on will help a great deal.

Choosing Permanent Colors

When choosing colors, keep in mind the areas that cannot readily be changed. *Anything permanent in your house should be chosen with care.* For instance, you can add lots of color in your wallpaper, paint, draperies and towels. The tile, countertops, appliances, and plumbing fixtures stay for a *long* time.

The little things that you never noticed before suddenly loom as major decisions. I remember becoming aware of the hardware on cabinets in homes, offices and restaurants wherever my husband and I went, thinking "Does this knob or handle look as though it is easy to use on a drawer or door?" At times we found ourselves driving around on scouting trips looking at the available colors of roofs, shutters and siding on homes, not to mention the styles of entrance ways, garage doors and dormers. Our builder would ask us about a style of "whatever," and we would comparison-shop. Of course, after we finally moved into our house, we often wondered why we drove ourselves absolutely mad over some of these details.

Carry your house plans with you at all times. They are now an essential part of you. As soon as you don't have them, you will be on an errand and wish you did. Always carry a ruler or small tape measure since you will be constantly checking sizes of rooms, windows and distances throughout the house. As time goes on, this portable packet grows to include paint color samples, cabinet colors, tile colors and carpeting colors, among other things.

Write everything down and keep a file. Keep a copy of any research you do or information you acquire. As soon as you throw away some scrap of paper, you'll find you will need it, or the person you gave the information to lost it, or that person cannot remember ever having had the information in the first place.

Keep a file on prices too. Deletions or additions to your home should be documented because ultimately they will affect the settlement price. Your house is probably not the only project the builder has to think about, so you must take the responsibility of record-keeping as well. Any changes that are made should be signed by yourself and the builder.

Settlement Day

On settlement day take your complete file along with you and have all your costs outlined. Make sure your settlement attorney arranges to withold a sum of money to cover any work your builder or subcontractors have left undone. If there is anything that needs to be reordered, repaired or finished in any way, the contractors and builder have a lot more incentive to complete the job to your satisfaction if they are waiting for final payment. You can agree on a reasonable sum of money in proportion to the amount of work involved. It is suggested to obtain a lawyer for closing on any house, whether you are in the situation of buying, selling or building.

Noteworthy Additions for Investment and or Resale

1. eye-catching front door and entry
2. exterior—good quality material such as brick, stone or wood
3. vestibule and ample foyer
4. kitchens—attractive with quality appliances, including a microwave
5. bathrooms—currently in fashion: the old-fashioned look in hardware, commodes, bathtubs and sinks
6. large closets—many devices available today to organize closets and make full use of your space
7. garage and basement—ample
8. washer/dryer—laundry room pleasant and convenient
9. good quality woodwork, cabinets, bookshelves
10. hardwood floors
11. cathedral ceilings
12. fireplaces
13. great room, and/or additional special purpose rooms, such as a den, sewing room or nursery
14. dead-bolt locks
15. security system
16. fire alarm/smoke detectors
17. large, interesting windows

Improvements—Poor Return on Investment

1. swimming pool
2. outside ground entrance to basement
3. finished basement
4. electronic gadgets

Generally speaking, homes today should be easy to maintain, not only to make life easier but also to serve as a good selling point.

9

REAL ESTATE AGENTS AND MORTGAGES

Selecting a Real Estate Agent

When you have established in your own mind what you want in a dwelling, then you need to embark on selecting a real estate agent. Select one recommended by *several* people, preferably people who have rented, bought or sold homes *recently* through the agent or the agency. Ideally, the real estate agent and the agency should belong to the multiple listing service in order to have access to listings from other companies. An added bonus in real estate agent qualifications would be an agent with a CRS degree (Certified Residential Specialist). These agents are local *residential specialists* who know your market and are up-to-date on the latest techniques and trends affecting the real estate industry.

Ask your real estate agent some questions to find out what he or she will do for you in the transaction. Will their agency be representing you, the seller or the lessor? What obligation will the agency have to you? The real estate agent's reputation in the community is his or her best reference, and since agents are very important to your transaction, you want to feel comfortable with them. Try to spend some time talking to your real estate agent when you are not actually looking at houses, such as over a casual lunch. This will help the agent learn more about your family and your family's needs, thereby satisfying your housing requirements more thoroughly. You in turn can appraise the agent's ability to meet your goals.

If you are not satisfied with the real estate agent's effort and

37

presentation, do not hesitate to contact someone from another agency. Last, but not least, real estate agencies have access to excellent city maps. Be sure to obtain one and take time to acquaint yourself with the map *before* you move to your new area.

Mortgage Rates

Your real estate agent should be aware of the mortgage rates and sources of loan money in your new community, but you should assume some of the responsibility for gathering this information on your own. Check with local banks and mortgage companies and compare the loan rates.

As you compare mortgage rates, note the differences in the additional costs such as legal fees, appraisal fees, title insurance fees, prepayment penalties and points (fees by the lender, one point equals one percent of the mortgage amount). All of these will figure into your estimates as well as the interest rate that is quoted. Take a calculator with you for quick estimates on your own.

Types of Loans and Mortgages

A real estate agent can give you more detailed information on the pros and cons of loans and mortgages available in your new location. Types frequently used are:

1. Federal Housing Administration (FHA) and government bond programs, which often offer loans with lower interest rates and a smaller down payment.
2. Assumable loans that may be held by a seller. These can be assumed by the new owner, often at a good interest rate. If the seller buys a condominium for $60,000 and sells it to you for $68,000 with an assumable loan, you pay the seller the $8,000 difference plus the seller's equity and then you assume the balance of the loan.
3. Conventional loan. This is a fixed-rate mortgage, which means the interest rate cannot change over the period of the loan.
4. Adjustable mortgage, which means the interest rate can fluctuate.

Request information *as early as possible* from your real estate agent on the closing costs *common to the state* into which you are moving. This is important because if you are relocating with a corporation you can negotiate the payment of these costs before mortgage shopping.

The price range on the house you buy will be established by the equity you have for a down payment, and your financial situation, will dictate the size of the mortgage you can qualify for. Twenty-eight percent of your gross income is generally an acceptable figure to use to determine how much house you can afford. However, a high debt ratio and considerable fixed debts will make a difference for loan qualification. Views are changing on the 28 percent figure. Qualification depends more and more on the buyer's marital status, financial status, employment and the housing market. When considering people as loan candidates, some lenders regard singles with no children and fewer financial obligations as reliable as couples.

Prequalifying and Preapproval

Generally people shop for a home first and then the mortgage. Consider reversing this order. Do your mortgage shopping first so you will have a more realistic idea of what is available in mortgage money and terms, as well as the amount of mortgage you qualify for. This is called "prequalifying," and the real estate agent can now approach the seller telling them: "Based on information the buyer has given the lender, the buyer has been prequalified for a mortgage for a certain dollar amount."

If you can obtain "preapproval," this will mean you are assured financing for a certain dollar amount on an appropriate property. This gives you more bargaining power and the advantage of shopping for homes directly in line with the amount of money you can afford.

These two conditions do not eliminate the mortgage contingency clause and you cannot finalize a sales contract on this basis. Check with the institutions that provide mortgages or a real estate agent for the latest information and the full advantages concerning these methods.

Buying Without a Down Payment

This article by Joe Kilsheimer of *The Orlando Sentinel* gives some great suggestions for buying a house without a down payment.

It has become an all too familiar problem. You want to buy a house, but you can't afford the down payment.

A recent report by the MIT-Harvard Joint Center for Housing Studies shows just how widespread the problem is. The report stated 81 percent of the estimated 11.1 million households aged 25 to 34 in 1986 did not have enough accumulated wealth to put a down payment on a first home.

Some suggestions: (1) Lease-option, the buyer agrees to lease the seller's house for a period, paying a fair rent with an option to buy and the rent being applied to the down payment. (2) Sweat equity, being allowed to finish work on the house, crediting the valuetoward the down payment. (3) Look for houses for sale by owner. Often you can negotiate more with these owners. (4) Transfer of tangible personal assets. You might have a boat, a car, jewelry or some other personal item that a seller might be willing to accept as a down payment. For lenders to approve this, you must get the item appraised and sign a bill of sale transferring the item at closing.

Negotiating the Transaction

Remember, the transaction is *always* negotiable. Whether you are renting or buying a dwelling, you can negotiate some areas. There is generally more bargaining with a purchase, but rentals may lend themselves to negotiations. Sometimes people will live in a dwelling at a reduced rental rate or rent-free in exchange for doing repair work. You can possibly negotiate to perform some other services for a reduction in rent, such as guarding an adjacent property for the owners or storing some of their furniture in the rental home for them.

If you find a property you like and are making an offer on it, make sure that the home is in good condition and that necessary repairs are completed or noted. Needed repairs are excellent negotiating points. The following list gives you more examples of negotiable items in a home purchase:

- Appliances, and whether they should be included in the price of the home. If there is concern about the home, appliances, heater, wiring or plumbing being sound, you can request a "buyer warranty plan." This plan will guarantee those major items, usually for one year.
- Payment of a buyer warranty plan is a negotiating point between the buyer and the seller.
- Objects difficult to move: fixtures, draperies or any large object, such as a pool table or large piano.
- Necessary replacements such as carpeting, tile or vinyl.
- Structural replacements or repair to the house.
- Closing costs between the buyer and seller (if the seller is anxious to make a sale, they may offer to pay some or all of the closing costs to make the transaction more attractive).

Details that you are negotiating must be outlined in the contract. These details make a difference in the price offered for the home. If possible, find out what the house was purchased for and what the houses in the neighborhood have been selling for. What is the situation of the people from whom you will be buying the house? How anxious are they to leave? Do they have other financial liabilities, such as a newly purchased home for a projected move of their own? In this case they may be intent on making a quick sale. Is the home well cared for? If not, the lack of care will probably be reflected in the care of the appliances and equipment left in the home. Is it a buyer's market or a seller's market? Gauge your bid accordingly. In a "down market" you can usually buy a house that is worth more than it is priced at, which means you can probably buy a house with not only your basic necessities but also one with some extra features. Real estate agents refer to this as adjusting your needs and wants list.

Note: Real estate agents with a CRS designation constitute 2% of all realtors. These agents are Graduates of the Realtors Institute (GRI) and have obtained certification by the National Association of Realtors.

LET'S SEE, PEDIATRICIAN, NEUROLOGIST GYNECOLOGIST, ENDOCRINOLOGIST, AND ORTHODONTIST. NOW ALL WERE MISSING IS THE ALLERGIST AND OUR HEALTH INSURANCE REPRESENTATIVE!

10

SELECTING QUALITY MEDICAL AND DENTAL CARE

Preventive medicine is still the best medicine. Give ample thought and preparation to future health care, even if you are blessed with good health. However, if you or a member of your family has a specific health problem, this chapter will be of special interest.

At one particular time, relocating our family required finding the following new doctors: pediatrician, neurologist, endocrinologist, orthopod, gynecologist, dentist, orthodontist, and allergist! I found it is always a good idea to give your specialists permission in writing to forward all medical records to your new doctor. When you find a doctor, he or she can readily obtain all the necessary records and treat your family more effectively.

Medical Records—Preparation for a Move

Retain doctors', dentists', and pharmacists' addresses and telephone numbers, even if you are moving out of the state or out of the country. You may need information on a health condition, treatment or medication clarification. Take pertinent medical and dental records with you as you travel to your new location, especially records for conditions that could have dire consequences: a heart condition, diabetes or a drug allergy, such as an allergy to penicillin. Take insurance forms with you, in case of an emergency.

Questions to Ask to Obtain a New Doctor

First of all, does the doctor speak your language? Will the doctor accept the medical insurance that your family has, be accessible to you and your home, be affiliated with a good hospital with diverse services, and have good qualifications? Specific problems you or your family have could require the services of a doctor or dentist with a speciality.

Most important: Do you feel comfortable with the doctor? A relationship with any doctor is personal, and you want to be able to talk freely with the doctor so he or she can have adequate information to treat your family properly.

Teaching institutions often have excellent quality internship and residency programs. As you are reviewing a new doctor's credentials, check to see what hospitals the doctor was associated with and what degrees he or she has obtained.

If you presently have a doctor whom you like and believe to be competent, you can ask for a referral for your new place of residence. Your doctor may have a friend or colleague near your new town, or your doctor may recommend a physician known through a professional medical organization.

Prescription Medicines and Pharmacy Records

A comprehensive checklist is in the back of the book for medications and their precautions in moving. The list will apply to moves within the United States as well as international moves. This is a very important topic, especially if one member of your family has a condition that requires special medications. *It is important to be familiar with your own prescription medications and their side effects.* Doctors strongly suggest that you wear an identification bracelet or neck chain on your body for special medical conditions, such as diabetes, heart condition or severe allergy.

International Preparation for Medical Assistance

Be aware of procedures for emergencies in any foreign country which you are visiting or relocating to. We had an experience that required emergency room treatment (at three a.m.) shortly after our arrival in England. We were staying in a flat instead of a hotel where we could have obtained assistance more easily. We didn't know the correct procedure to reach a telephone operator (in England you must dial 100), let alone know the hospital casualty ward (emergency room) locations. We also found out that not all hospitals in England have these wards! The route to the hospital and driving procedures were uncharted ground for us. Luckily, it was not a life-threatening situation, but it could have been.

Before moving to another country, be sure you have information on common medical procedures and how to obtain them. Know where hospitals and doctors are located, and map out the routes to these facilities or offices. It is helpful to know the generic name of prescription drugs you are using so that prescriptions can be duplicated more easily. Drugs are usually the same or similar in different countries, but they are known by different trade names.

Do You Need Information on How to Find a New Doctor or a New Dentist?

The following sources contain excellent information to obtain quality health care in the United States and in Europe. Physicians and hospitals everywhere are making a sincere effort to promote public awareness of this topic.

1. *A Guide to Selecting Quality Health Care.* This booklet can be obtained by sending a self-addressed, stamped envelope to Center for Health Affairs, Two Wisconsin Circle, Suite 500, Chevy Chase, MD 20815.

2. *How to Select the Right Doctor.* A 15-page brochure, free from Georgetown Medical Directory, 2233 Wisconsin Avenue, N.W., Suite 333, Washington, DC 20007.

3. **Physician Finder Service.** Many hospitals have these services and they usually suggest three doctors in a particular field of medicine; they also list the physicians' years of experience, specialties, subspecialties, age, sex, and anything that is pertinent to your situation. Many doctor referral programs also are available today in many cities. To contact them, call the 1-800 operator for the doctor referral service in your area, or check with your local hospital.

4. **Selecting a Dentist in the United States.** Anthony P. Abdalla, D.M.D., P.C., Allentown, Pennsylvania, suggested these sources for information on obtaining a new dentist as you relocate.

- Dental schools, primarily for people moving into a major metropolitan area
- Dental specialists such as periodontist, endodontist or oral surgeon
- Medical doctor

5. **International Association for Medical Assistance for Travelers.** This is an excellent contact when planning to travel abroad. Call (716) 754-4883 or write to IAMAT at 417 Center Street, Lewiston, NY 14092. Although membership in this nonprofit organization is free, the association gratefully accepts donations to continue their research work. An annual directory lists 500 IAMAT centers. These centers are all over the world and can provide you with English- or French-speaking doctors and numerous other benefits of membership.

6. **Dental Information—International.** The guidelines presented for United States relocation from Dr. Abdalla will apply when you travel or relocate abroad.

Many doctors and dentists are obtained by referrals from friends and colleagues. Anyone whose credibility and judgment you trust could be a source of information.

> * Note the checklist for medical and dental in the back of the book.

11

EVALUATING AND SELECTING SCHOOLS

Criteria to Select a School

Selecting the best possible school system for your family is a challenge in itself. *A school should provide a complete education!* You must take into consideration the student's individual educational requirements, abilities and interests, present and future. The quality of education is a prime concern, but the overall atmosphere of the school must be conducive to allowing your student to learn and absorb the material presented to him or her. Some important areas to consider:

- language and math instruction
- atmosphere and activities of the school
- the overall philosophy, values and policies of the school
- the size of the classes
- the teacher-pupil ratio
- the construction of the school
- the comfort of the classrooms

When you are relocating, there are so many tasks to complete that it may be good to take your high school student with you on a school-shopping trip. Students will focus on the school, whereas you have many other thoughts and tasks running through your head. Students will quickly pick up on the atmosphere inside and outside of the schools because they are in more familiar territory.

47

A booklet I highly recommend is **Choosing a School for Your Child**. This booklet has comprehensive information and guidelines for selecting a school. **Choosing a School for Your Child** is printed by the U.S. Department of Education.

1. For a free copy write to Choosing a School, Consumer Information Center, Pueblo, CO 81009

2. This booklet is also available from ERIC Document Reproduction Service (EDRS), 3900 Wheeler Ave., Alexandria, VA 22304. (Order #ED-302872, Microfiche $0.86, paper copy $2.03.)

The following guidelines for selecting a school system are made by Charles Knapp, a counselor at Allen High School in Allentown, Pennsylvania.

> You must always consider the individual needs of your children and their areas of interest. The school should have a diversity of programs, offering musical programs, fine arts, honors programs, and adequate sports facilities, for example. Individual sports are also very important. The academic standards must be considered as well as the number of National Merit Scholars from that school. SAT scores and computer instruction are important.

As you are school shopping, consider these points and inquire about the school's academic test evaluation results. These test scores should be available to you. Any good school will be proud to share them with you.

Having had three children attend three different colleges, my husband and I believe that the percentage of students from the high school applying to and being accepted by a college is very important. So too is the caliber of these colleges. Obtain information on the student achievement after enrollment, if it is available. Some high school counselors are aware of how their former students are performing in college.

The following tips are from Mary Omdahl, of RE/MAX 100 Real Estate in Allentown, Pennsylvania.

> To find the best school system when moving to a new area, subscribe to local newspapers and follow school activities and budget news. Area colleges with teacher education programs may also recommend which school systems are good. Also, call county or state departments

of education for results of standardized tests, which are broken down by school systems.

School Considerations—Prior to Moving

Before moving, visit the present school and obtain the names and descriptions of the books and readers your children are using so that the new teacher will have an idea of your children's curriculum. Have any special programs outlined, so that you can check the availability of the same in your new area. Spend time with each child's teacher so you are aware of anything he or she considers to be of value about your student to pass along to the new teacher. Grades and achievements can be sent to the new school or given to you to deliver personally, depending on relocation timing.

International School Systems

International moves require a particularly careful examination of the academic program since many foreign assignments are temporary. *You must make sure your daughter or son will have the courses needed to return to school in the United States.* International schools may enjoy a fine academic program, but they may vary considerably from the U.S. schools in their social and athletic programs. You and your children should visit the international school and spend time with a counselor or other school representative. Consult with colleagues and friends also on assignment to the country to which you are moving and discuss their experiences with the schools in the area.

Types of International Schools and Costs

Two of the more well-known school systems in Europe are the American Community Schools and TASIS Schools. These schools are excellent academically and fully accredited. They also offer diverse sports programs. They manage to mix the activities their students have been accustomed to while adding an international flair to the student's school experience. The schools offer students living abroad the flexibility they need as their families move from country to country. International moves at times involve more than one country, as the employee may be relocated to several countries before returning to America.

Costs of the international schools are an important consideration, since the schools are expensive. Many corporations include school costs as a part of the employee relocation package, due to the fact that there are few options for relocated students to continue their education with school courses that are necessary in their curriculum.

It is imperative to correlate each student's completed U.S. academic courses with those offered abroad. As I stressed earlier, you should be certain that the student will receive the required courses in the international school for a successful matriculation when returning to the United States.

International Boarding Schools

Boarding schools abroad are another alternative. If you consider these schools, be sure to spend adequate time with your student and the school advisor going over all the details of the school. Know what is expected of your child academically as well as what the student's daily life will be like. The boarding school regimen is quite different, strict and very demanding, and the curriculum is more likely geared toward the country that you are residing in. This experience might be too much of a cultural change for your child and should therefore be carefully evaluated.

12

CONSIDERATIONS FOR CHILDREN

This chapter is written at the suggestion of our daughter, Amy, who is a Pennsylvania State University graduate living and working in Boston. As another stalwart member of my family who graciously read my manuscript, she reminded me of the difficulties that children can experience during relocation and how hard it can be for some children to make changes in their schools and their friends.

Moving can be a positive and a growing experience and it can also be a difficult experience. Most children will adjust to a new situation in time with patience and understanding, but you should be aware that problems can arise from uprooting children from one environment and placing them in another.

Avoiding Common Problems

Children may feel lost or believe they are losing their identity when a move takes place. They may feel sad leaving their "best friend in all the world," so you should assure your children that they can have exchange visits with their friends the following summer or during a school break (if practical). Help your children write to their friends and suggest an occasional phone call on weekends. This will give them something to look forward to and make the farewells a little easier. Some children may be more affected by a move than others, depending on their age, their personality or the activities they are involved in at school, in church or around the neighborhood.

51

As you plan your move, consider relocating near the end of the summer (if you have a choice), especially if your children are involved in a lot of summer functions or sports. Summer spent in a new area with few friends and activities can be difficult.

Very young children will adapt to a new situation more easily if their daily routine is not changed. These children do not have many outside influences as their associations are with parents and their immediate surroundings. As children mature and become more involved, they start to identify with friends and activities and it may be more difficult for them to make a change. Children also worry about a lot of things that we, as adults, would think trivial. Second graders, for instance, may worry that they will not board the right school bus, not find their room in the new school, or not get off the bus at the right stop on the way home. They may be afraid the new children will not like them as much as their former friends. Different ages and circumstances may produce different anxieties for your children.

The best you can do as parents is to communicate daily with your children. Let each child know that you do understand his or her feelings and that those feelings are very important to you. Talk about their daily activities and be aware of their concerns. Attempt as much as possible, to instill confidence in your children and to help them acquire self-esteem. Anyone with confidence and self-esteem will adjust more easily in new situations and new environments.

Your children should know you will be making an effort as a family to make the move a positive experience for everyone. Explain the job circumstances carefully, with as much detail as each child's age permits, and further explain that you are moving as a family and how necessary it is to support each other. Whenever you can, involve your children in decisions and moving plans, so they will know what to expect, and what is expected of them.

If it is possible, take your children to the new town prior to, in conjunction with, or after finding a house in order to show them something of the area. This will help dispel their apprehension about relocating. If time permits, show them some of the city's highlights and anything that will be significant to their life in the new area..

Behavioral Changes
(Those Signifying Problems)

As parents you should be cognizant of changes in your child's daily habits and attitudes. It is not easy for many of us to put our feelings into words, especially if we are upset and do not even know why we are feeling the way that we do. Expressing feelings articulately is even more difficult for a child.

Reading problems are usually the *first* indication that a child is upset. Sudden reading difficulties should be investigated *quickly*. If a child develops a reading problem, other academic subjects will suffer, since all subjects hinge on reading skills to some extent. Other indicators include changes in attention span, eating habits (such as weight loss), study habits, enthusiasm, energy levels, relationships with you or siblings and sleep patterns.

You can also inform the schoolteacher of problems you believe the child is experiencing. A teacher can give new students a little extra attention or a special assignment to make them feel more welcome. Teachers encounter new students so often that they are usually willing and able to help the newcomers adjust. Teachers should know, however, if you are witnessing behavioral changes at home. Children may appear to be doing very well in school, and then let their true feelings show only at home.

The temptation, as you are moving into a new home, is to get settled as quickly as possible so you will feel comfortable and regulated in your surroundings. As important as that is, you must take time with your children to talk about their feelings and their daily activities. Watch carefully for insidious changes and address those changes before they become more of a problem than they deserve to be.

Allow your children time to adjust. It is all right for a child to drop back a bit and not get involved in too many activities immediately. Sometimes it is better to sort out a new and different situation, and then become selectively involved in the new school and the new community.

At the end of the day, relocating children can have a happy ending. Whenever a person encounters difficulty in life and conquers the situation on a positive note, the person ultimately becomes stronger for the effort. It may not be our desire to move to a new location, but the fact is that more and more people are moving for one reason or another than ever before. So pay close attention, and treat the children with consideration and a bit of tender loving care.

* Note the free brochure from American Movers Conference called *Moving and Children* in Chapter 17 in the section on AMC.

13

ANIMALS HAVE FEELINGS TOO

For the most part, the animals my family acquired always seemed to have conveniently followed our children home, although there was the odd one or two that we actually purchased. Living with us, our animals had to be flexible as they ultimately became as well traveled as we were.

We had one particular cat named Clementine who made many moves with us. During one of those moves she became scared by all the movers and activity, and when the truck and movers finally departed at nine p.m. in the pouring rain, Clementine was nowhere to be found. Our children were safely ensconced at my parent's home, a five-hour drive away, but we knew we could not arrive the next day without Clem. So my husband, who never liked cats anyway, trudged around outside with a large umbrella calling for the cat. Finally, when she didn't turn up, he said a little prayer to St. Anthony (anyone who attended Catholic grade school will know it) and, lo and behold, Clementine came bouncing down the hill with her collar tags tinkling away.

I will not mention the other dogs and cats we had, but with all the moves, suffice it to say there were enough. One dog left after I threatened "It's that dog or me." It was a fairly safe assumption on my part that I would be the one to stay, because the dog could not cook and she never did learn to drive.

Preparing an Animal for a Move

Before moving, be sure to contact your veterinarian for your pet's health records. *All* the animal's shots should be up-to-date. Before departing, acquire an identification tag for your pet with the new address. If you are unable to take care of this before leaving, get a new address tag as soon as possible upon arrival in the new city, along with local tags from the town or county in which you will be residing. Animals can become confused and lost in a new area, so it is important for them to have identification tags.

Travel Equipment for Your Pet

On the day of departure be sure to take enough food and

water for your pet, enough to last the duration of the trip. Pets as well as people can develop an upset stomach from new water, something you definately want to avoid. It is also easier to stop for nourishment for people rather than for animals. Pack your pet's leash and a toy or two. Wherever you travel, have someone walk your pet frequently so the animal can get oriented to its new surroundings. This helps the pet avoid "accidents." Proper pet preparation will help your relocation trip proceed smoothly.

International Preparation

International moves including pets are more involved. Your moving company will have information on the procedures to follow to transport your pet abroad. The type of traveling kennel, required vaccinations, forms and diet details should be outlined for you. Standard specifications for an adequately sized portable kennel in which your pet can travel say the pet must be able to stand up, turn around and lie down in natural positions. Diet restrictions usually include no solid food the day of departure and ample water in the kennel for the trip. Airline travel arrangements should be made in advance to assure space for your pet.

For an international move, your pet should be in good health to make the transition (preferably on the advice of a veterinarian), and you should know the rules and regulations for pets entering another country. If your pet must be in quarantine for six months, as in England, check the boarding kennels yourself or have a reliable person do it for you. Our venture into kennel shopping for our dog Duff made us realize that boarding conditions varied considerably. Some kennels have more caring help and better-kept facilities, including a veterinarian (or several) on staff. Also, the length of travel time from your home to the kennel is a consideration, as you will be visiting your pet frequently for the purpose of building everyone's morale—yours, the children's and your pet's.

* Note the checklist for pets in the back of the book.

14

CULTURE SHOCK

Culture is defined as the development of the mind and the body by education and training. Our culture therefore is all that we are, do, feel and experience. It embodies our surroundings, our friends and the very essence of our life. We are constantly bombarded by messages of what we are and what we are about.

When people are physically removed from their cozy, secure existence and transplanted into another culture, the changes can be traumatizing. Some people are more affected by change than others. Sometimes moving from one section of a city to another is a dramatic change, causing culture shock; the outcome depends on the individual and the circumstances.

Cultural change means obtaining new and unfamiliar responses to old and familiar habits. Removing our routine signals, and replacing them with other signals, can be disturbing and stressful. We are now struggling to find appropriate ways to react to a situation that was at one time routine and normal for us. I am sure we have all experienced cultural change when traveling to new areas on holiday; however, after a trip is over, we return home and laugh it off as just another experience. If you are now "home" and still getting these different signals, there is nowhere to go for the old and familiar responses.

Symptoms

Culture shock can manifest itself in feelings ranging from mild apathy to severe anxiety. Although culture shock is usu-

59

ally a passing phase, one should know its signs and symptoms, know that it will pass and be aware of methods to ease the transition.

Recognizing culture shock for what it is, is a positive step. Culture shock may display itself in many forms—difficulty in sleeping, headaches, stomachaches, impatience, anxiety and possibly anger. These feelings can and do pass with time and effort. If these symptoms do not disappear in a reasonable amount of time, you may consider seeing a physician in case the symptoms signify a physical problem.

Methods to Master

One coping method is to make your life in a new area as pleasant as possible. In each residence (no matter how temporary), try to set up your living quarters as comfortably as you can with a few pictures, a few mementos and possibly some colorful houseplants around you. This will give you a measure of comfort in a new environment. Try to find as many positive aspects to your new city as you can. Whatever you do, don't sit home alone and brood. Get out, make new friends and join an organization to meet or help people.

This is *key support plus* time for everyone in the family. You must be able to talk to each other, or to someone who is empathetic, and be able to moan a little now and then. Call a friend from your former place of residence. Call on the weekend when the rate is low and treat yourself to some quality time with a friend. Consider the cost of the phone call as a lunch with your friend. Anyone in transition needs help and support; however, one must occasionally make an attempt at pulling oneself up by the bootstraps.

Usually it takes six to 10 months until someone begins to feel at home in a new environment. The amount of time varies and is proportionate to the individual, the area and the events taking place in one's life at the time of the move. If the feelings of homesickness do not pass, a trip back to your former home may help. This in fact may make you look at the former area in a new perspective and cause you to look forward to returning to your new city. When this occurs, you will start to realize that you are over the culture shock—or nearly over it, anyway.

Preparation time for the employee and their family is a good investment by employers. Ample preparation is necessary for moves to be successful, nationally and internationally. It has been documented that the costly failures of corporate moves are primarily because the family, the spouse especially, does not adjust to the new situation.

Relocation preparation comes best in the form of advice on planning a move and all that it entails, including information on the new city, state or country. The help that is given will foster goodwill and make the company/employee/family relationship stronger and more meaningful. And in the long run, will be substantially more cost-effective.

Some of the points made in this chapter are derived in part from the study by Nancy J. Adler, *International Dimensions of Organizational Behavior*, 2nd ed. (Boston: PWS-Kent Publishing Company, 1991), p.229, 274.

Enjoy the scenery as you travel the detour,
or as my friend Noreen Beggy says,
*"Life is what happens to you
while you are making other plans."*

15

MAKE THE BEST OF YOUR MOVE

Whenever we were in the process of moving to a new home, my husband and I planned the travel route to include unusual or special sites located along the way. At times we deviated from the most efficient route so we could see what a particular city, town or state had to offer. These special sites included anything fun, educational or generally of interest to our family. Relocating in this way enables a family to transform a move into a minivacation and add an extra dimension to the trip. *Seeing sights along the way as you travel to a new location takes less time than you may think.*

Explore the city or country that you move into as much as possible. An added bonus of a relocation is that it allows your family to study whatever part of the country you are currently residing in. This is an on-the-spot geography lesson.

There were times we lived in an area for such a short period that we found ourselves hurrying around to catch all the wondrous sights before we packed our possessions and departed. The move that spanned only four months in California was the real challenge. Before we left the state we managed to travel from our home near Los Angeles to San Francisco during the only four-day holiday available, Thanksgiving weekend. We had our noon meal in Chinatown on Turkey Day; however, the family still believed we should have a turkey dinner with all the trimmings before the day was complete. Denny's Restaurant was the only restaurant that we felt comfortable taking five well-traveled people to for dinner. But as it was very late in the day, Denny's had used the last serving of turkey just before we ordered our meal. This was a minor inconvenience, because we did have a marvelous time that weekend.

As a result of our many moves, we have managed to see some wonderful cities and sights. On our journeys we traveled through 38 states and countless foreign countries. My husband, Stan, is a graduate of the United States Naval Academy, and after graduation he served in the U.S. Navy's Nuclear Submarine Service, which afforded us numerous moves, mostly up and down the East Coast. Upon leaving the service (supposedly to settle down), he began work with a company in eastern Pennsylvania, and we were on the move again. During most of this time we were all too busy to analyze whether we were enjoying the scenery along the detour. In retrospect, I believe we did, although Chris, our youngest, was too small to appreciate many of the places. When we mention some of the highlights of our moves, we say, "Yes, you were there." He was at least two or three years of age; he should remember.

One of our most delightful moves came just as we thought we were comfortably settled into what we expected to be our last home. We were asked to take an assignment in Europe, and after much discussion we decided it would be a nice opportunity in many respects. At the time only our youngest son was living at home. Chris finished school abroad and in so doing gained many fine experiences. The time we spent in Europe added a new dimension to family travels. The countries we visited and the experiences we had are a treasure trove of memories. We decided the time spent living abroad would be temporary, and we set out to make the most of it.

Any move, whether in America or to a foreign country, can and should be a chance to expand your individual and your family's horizons. Always consider a move a growing experience and "enjoy the scenery as you travel the detour."

16

FINAL WEEK BEFORE DEPARTURE

This is the week to check all the last-minute details in your lists, files and survival boxes. Go through your home, noting the furniture, fabric or anthing else you will need to reference for color before moving into your new home.

Organizing Rooms—Labeling for Packing

Organize your small and easily transportable furniture before the moving company personnel arrive. It may seem trivial to rearrange pieces so soon but remember that it does save valuable time when moving into the new home. For one thing, there are always four or five (or perhaps more) people asking you where to place all the items as you move in.

The organization I am referring to, pertains mainly to lamps, pictures and small appointments that you can mentally rearrange, easily move and then have packed accordingly. These boxes will then automatically be labeled and placed in the appropriate room or area in the new home.

Make last-minute notes on what you need from each room. If you desire to pack some articles yourself, the moving company will deliver boxes ahead of time if you request it. I recommend packing anything you may need immediately, such as personal clothing, bedding or bathtowels. You can then mark the boxes yourself for easy reference.

For insurance purposes, it is advisable to have the moving company pack breakable or (large) valuable items Separate and label items before the movers arrive. Ask them to label

STAN, I FOUND THOSE
DIAPERS WE'VE BEEN
MISSING!

boxes specifically, such as "John's bedding" instead of just "linens," which can mean various things.

Label anything not to be packed. You can even store items in the trunk of your automobile so these do not inadvertently get put into cartons. Despite labeling, things can go awry. During an early move, we had a growing pile of equipment to take with us, including clean diapers, baby food, our own clothes, baby equipment and some things to be laundered, including a bag of soiled diapers, all labeled with a big sign "Do Not Pack." You guessed it. They packed the whole thing. By the time we arrived at our new destination, the soiled diapers were really ripe, to say the least. Although the diapers we used 27 years ago are no longer a problem (Do I hear a sigh of relief?), the point here is that it is very important to be aware of the moving process at all times. This is why you need assistance from family or friends on this day. Mistakes can and do happen at this hectic time.

Pictures Serve as Reference

If your household goods are going into storage or will in some way be unavailable to you, it's a good idea to take pictures of your furniture, bedspreads, lamps, area carpets or anything that you may want to reference for colors. You may want to shop for drapes, blinds, carpeting or paint before you move into the new home, and it is very helpful to have these colors available in snapshots rather than trusting them to memory.

Appliance Preparation

The following tips remind you of everyday items that always need care in a move. If you have other equipment in your home or apartment, check the equipment manuals for service and care advice.

1. Clean and defrost the refrigerator.
   Take a small box of baking soda, cut the box open and wrap the box with a thin piece of cloth. Store this in the refrigerator to deter odors for several months. An alternative method is to put charcoal in a loose cloth. Wipe the whole inside of the refrigerator with vinegar to avoid any mildew buildup.
2. Clean the oven and the range.
3. Drain the washing machine *well*.
4. Clean the dishwasher and remove all leftover soap.
5. Grind a lemon (cut into pieces) into your garbage disposal to eliminate odors.
6. Dry the interiors of all your appliances.

Equipment such as stereo equipment should be packed according to the directions in the manuals, and preferably in their own cartons. Check your storage areas for these boxes before the movers arrive.

Departure Day

You have planned the move as much as you can. Now it is a matter of rechecking your organization, the survival boxes, your file for important papers and the "Do Not Pack" signs to be sure everything is ready.

When the movers arrive, begin with introductions, and proceed to escort them through the house, acquainting them with the home and all your messages. Mention travel times and schedules at the outset. You may have a deadline for your place of lodging after the house is empty, and the movers may have a schedule to meet too. It is important to take this time to be sure you and the movers have a clear understanding of what must be accomplished and in what time frame. Never assume anything in life (and especially in a move).

As a mover finishes packing one room, request the boxes to be arranged in each room to facilitate easy cleaning. The sooner you begin your final sweep through the house, the better. Each time the movers finish a room, you can complete whatever cleaning remains. At the end of the day check closets and permanent cabinet drawers a second time. *Check them yourself!* Otherwise articles may be misplaced and left behind. Even after a room is finished, someone may inadvertently put something in an open drawer or an open closet, so it is advisable to double-check.

The very last thing to do, after the cleaning is complete, is to check all the appliances that will remain in the home. They should be set appropriately or turned off. Adjust the heater/ air conditioning gauge, close the windows, turn the lights off and lock the house. If you are moving before you have sold your home, see the vacant home instructions in the checklist for departure day.

Now on to your next challenge—the "moving-in" procedure. You can do it!

"STAN, HAVE YOU SEEN JIMMY, I CAN'T FIND HIM ANYWHERE?"

* Note the checklist for final week and departure day in the back of the book.

17

THE MOVERS ARE COMING

It isn't fair. No one ever said moving is fair. There are always more of them (the movers) than there are of us (the movees). That is always the way it is. No matter how you plan your day, it just works out that way. Aside from this fact of life, the movers always arrive at eight a.m. sharp, ready to charge.

There is a way to survive. ORGANIZE, ORGANIZE! That is our goal here. Everything that you have done in the way of organization up until now will expedite the move and thereby keep the costs down.

Just as we did when departing the former home, begin again with introductions and use the movers' names often. This is important. Personalize your move in this way and you will have a good working relationship with the movers for the day or days that they are with you. When the relationship is smooth, the whole moving process will function better. Next, take the time to show all the movers the entire home, acquainting them with the room plots as you go along. The room plots that we made earlier (Chapter 6, Furniture—Measuring to Scale), should be posted in each room. The moving personnel will appreciate not having to locate you whenever they need a decision on a piece of furniture. This will expedite the unloading and placement of furniture, saving your moving company man-hours, not to mention your own time and energy later.

"THE MOVERS ARE COMING,
THE MOVERS ARE COMING!"
*Take a deep breath and remember,
The best thing about the future is
that it comes only one day at a time.*

Orienting the Movers

Kim Hill, an experienced 26-year navy wife with many moves, offers this suggestion to orient movers to your new house: Decide ahead of time on the furniture arrangement and into which room each piece will be placed, then number the rooms and post the master list. As the movers come through the door with the furniture, give them the number of the room for that particular piece. This is helpful for large houses or a very complicated floor plan or, as is often the case, if you happen to be the only family member at home on moving day. This tip came from Kim on a move in August

1988 into Buchanan House at the United States Naval Academy. Kim's husband is Rear Admiral Virgil L. Hill, Jr., Superintendent of the U.S. Naval Academy. Buchanan House consists of 16,000 square feet, a little more than your average-size home!

Unpacking the Boxes

If you have professional movers, they will unpack some boxes if you desire. This is a tremendous help, especially with china and crystal. Glassware and dishes not frequently used can be washed later when time permits. This also will speed the removal of the seemingly endless number of boxes, which can be removed by the moving company.

Signing Your Moving Documents

After the goods are delivered to your home, the packing and inventory slips pertaining to the move must be signed. Note "subject to final inspection" on the form above your signature for unopened boxes and especially boxes with obvious dents. This way, if damages have occurred, you can claim them with less difficulty. *Know your company's requirements for claim procedures.*

American Movers Conference Consumer Programs

The American Movers Conference is the national trade association for the interstate household goods moving industry. AMC represents some 1,500 van lines and their agents throughout the United States.

AMC sponsors an arbitration program for consumers that is approved by the Interstate Commerce Commission and is operated by the American Arbitration Association. The program is open to AMC member companies whose participation is voluntary. It is limited to loss and damage claims on interstate moves.

AMC also provides free brochures on moving to consumers. Send a self-addressed, stamped business-size envelope to American Movers Conference, 2200 Mill Road, Alexandria, VA 22314. The brochures they offer are *Guide to a Satisfying Move, Moving and Children* and *Moving Your Pets and Plants.*

STAN ALWAYS HAD A WAY
OF ATTRACTING A FEW
DEPENDABLE PEOPLE

18

MOVING YOURSELF

Early Stage—Equipment Needed

Moving without a moving company requires the same organization mentioned in the previous chapters. However, this alternative will require more organization and packing on your part, and you will need to engage friends or relatives to assist you.

Start early by acquiring boxes from convenience stores, liquor stores or grocery stores. Liquor store boxes are excellent because they are sturdy and have partitions that give you added protection for glasses, vases and small breakable items. Used boxes can be purchased for a reasonable price from moving companies, and their wardrobe boxes are hard to improve on for practicality. The wardrobe boxes are strong, transport clothing well, and the bottom of the box can be utilized for sweaters or any other unbreakable, reasonably light items. Mattress boxes and kitchen barrels can also be purchased.

As soon as you know you are moving, begin to save whatever wrapping paper you can. Beware of wrapping items in newspaper as the ink will rub off. Newspaper nevertheless is good for padding the bottoms of boxes. Put aside old blankets and rope to wrap and secure the furniture. Stock up on package-sealing tape, marking pens and labels.

Self-help moving companies will have furniture ties and blankets for rent if you do not have some available. Dollies are another popular item that can be rented, and they are very helpful when moving heavy appliances.

These are all things that you should check into, especially if it is a busy moving season. Reserve a rental truck early so you have an adequate size. If you know the rooms of furniture that you have to move, a good company can suggest the size truck you'll need. If you are debating on the size, rent one a little larger rather than one a bit smaller than the estimate. It is difficult to assess all that you actually have in those drawers and closets. *Remember*—50 percent of all household moves are made between the last week in May and the first week in October. So plan ahead!

Organize the Help

Engage as much *dependable* help as you can. It is important to start on time to expedite the move, thereby avoiding costly delays. A two-hour delay could ultimately cost you an extra day's rental fee for the truck and/or equipment. Take some time with your helpers to go through the household items to be moved. Let everyone know what must be accomplished and the time frame you are working in. Packing the truck should be organized by *one person*, and the other assistants should be the "gofers."

NO HONEY, I SAID "GOFERS" NOT "GOPHERS"!!

Appliance Preparation

Check all the manuals on appliances for directions on preparing for the move. Washers, dryers and refrigerators require special care. Clean and defrost the refrigerator. Clean the oven and the range. Drain the washing machine *well*. Dry the interiors of all your appliances. Remove all the fittings and accessories and pack them in a plastic bag and tape the bag to the inside of the appliance. (See Chapter 16 for more details on appliance preparation.)

Stereo Equipment, Radio

Stereo equipment, radios, clocks, toasters and small appliances should be packed according to the directions in the owner's manuals and preferably in their own cartons if you have them.

Packing

Moving on your own takes more preparation, so be sure to start as soon as you can, packing anything that you can do without for a reasonable time. Start with items you know you will not be using. For instance, if you are making plans in February for a move in May, you can begin by packing the Christmas decorations. Pack and mark all breakables carefully. Wrap and pad pictures and mirrors well and pack in cardboard containers. Pack items inside every nook and cranny, such as the inside of appliances (refrigerator, washer and dryer), with light, unbreakable items. Remember to unpack these same appliances before use! Utilize all drawer space, also with lighter items and small pictures. Towels or sweaters can be wrapped around these objects.

Loading the Truck

Begin by loading the heavier furniture and appliances at the cab of the truck, packing it as tightly as possible. Tie strong rope around the furniture from one side of the truck to the other. Do this approximately every quarter of the truck capacity. The goal is to secure everything as well as possible. Some trucks have a special section for fragile items. Pictures and mirrors should be loaded on the truck sideways. Some can be packed in between the mattress and the boxspring. Heavy boxes of equal weight can be packed one on top of the other.

Preparing Houseplants

Place your plants in the truck last and store them carefully. A bookcase can be placed sideways at the back of the van and the plants placed in the open areas. Water the plants sparingly, then allow them to drain overnight so you do not have water leakage on cartons and furniture. If some vines or leaves get broken, simply trim them off when you arrive in your new location.

Rules of the Company!

Know the rules of the company from whom you are renting your truck and equipment in case problems occur on the road, such as a flat tire or mechanical malfunctions. *Have everything in writing* and know telephone numbers for service contacts and assistance.

Insurance Required

Check on the moving company's insurance coverage, and not only for the *truck and equipment but also for the contents.* Is it adequate, or will you need additional coverage? Your household inventory will help you assess the amount needed to cover your personal belongings. Check your personal insurance policy to determine coverage in case of accident to yourself or any volunteer helpers.

Many self-help moving companies publish excellent material to assist you in inventoring, estimating and organizing your move. The booklet called *Mover's Advantage* by Ryder Truck Rental, Incorporated, is a good example. This booklet can be obtained by calling 1-800-327-3399.

---

* Note the checklist for moving yourself in the back of the book.

19

ADJUSTING IN A NEW CITY

Getting Acquainted

New neighborhood, new school, new position and new friends. Wow! So much to consider and adjust to. This is where culture shock takes on meaning.

As you and your family are trying to adapt to a new situation, it will help all concerned if you occasionally tell each other about the difficulties you are experiencing. Do not dwell on the downside of the adjustments you are experiencing, but share your feelings with one another and thereby support each other. In so doing, you become closer as a family. You will realize that you are not the only family member feeling lonely or frustrated or both.

The person who is changing jobs does not always have an easy time of it either. Adjusting to a new situation, with new co-workers or a new staff accustomed to doing things a certain way for many years, is just one of the many challenges that person will encounter. I remember one time when my husband first became a district manager and had been in his position for about two weeks when he called the office one day to speak to his secretary.

"Hello, this is Stan. Are there any messages for me?"
The receptionist answered, "Stan who?"

What a letdown, to say the least!

Upon arriving in your new city, visit your local chamber of commerce or information bureau to find out what museums,

"HELLO THIS IS STAN, ARE THERE ANY MESSAGES FOR ME?"

"STAN WHO?"

theaters and events are nearby. To become familiar with the town, travel around the city with your family, and do some shopping or browsing.

Get acquainted with local driving regulations and other local laws in your new city, state or country. Before the first day of class, arrange to take your children to their new school to acquaint them with the surroundings (possibly showing them their classroom) and introduce them to any teachers who may be available. If you know where the bus stops are, show your children the way to them. This reduces first-day anxiety, a feeling particularly common in smaller children.

After you are settled in your new home, make an attempt

to become active in school and church functions or other organizations. It is an effective way to get to know people and make friends, and it will disperse lonely feelings. Check into adult education programs. If you don't find anything nearby that strikes your fancy, start a group or program of your own. My neighbors and I started a stock investment organization in one city, and it proved to be very interesting for everyone who participated.

Remember, most of the time *you will have to take the initiative* to meet new neighbors and to join groups or organizations. People do not typically come knocking at your door.

Make Yourself at Home

The following suggestions are steps you should accomplish early in a new location. These are taken from Ryder's *Mover's Advantage.*

1. Open new bank accounts; secure your valuables in a safe-deposit box.
2. Scout the neighborhood. Note the locations of local schools, restaurants, markets, hospitals, barber shops, beauty salons, dry cleaners and pharmacies.
3. Compile a service list. Begin to note who can supply home services (contractors, decorators, plumbers, gardeners) and personal services (doctors, dentists, lawyers, insurance agents, veterinarians).
4. Register to vote.
5. Send change-of-address notes to friends and relatives. A scenic postcard of the area makes for a nice note.

Arrange for basic services to begin, such as electricity, water, telephone, gas, trash collection and television cable. For some of these services, you must make plans to be home from eight a.m. until five p.m., so plan accordingly. Don't dash out for a quart of milk or you will come back to a sign on the door saying, "Sorry we missed you! Call the office for another appointment."

> * Note the checklist for new city in the back of the book.

PART II

INTERNATIONAL INFORMATION AND OTHER TOPICS

MATE, TELL ME YOU DIDN'T LET HIM PACK THOSE NAPPYS IN THE BOOT!

20

INTERNATIONAL RELOCATION

Making the Decision

If you have been selected as a candidate for an overseas assignment, you have many significant aspects to consider before making the decision. There will be many changes encountered by yourself and your family in foreign countries. These changes will be at work, at school and in your everyday activities. If possible, talk with people who have lived in the designated country. Do *as much* research as possible on all aspects of the job assignment, and specifically on the city and the country. Essential to the decision is how your family feels about the move.

It is very important in all moves to *know yourself* and what you are capable of as a person, as an employee and as a family member. In international moves, knowing yourself and what you can adjust to is critical. When we were asked to move to England in 1985, we thought we were well-prepared because we had been through the corporation's orientation program and because we had received tips from friends who had lived there. Additionally, our son was very enthusiastic about the prospect of living and learning in Europe. Many people said to us, "At least you all speak the same language."

On our move to England we found that visiting a country and living there are two entirely different experiences. We soon realized that Americans and the British do not speak the same language. For example:

American	British
drugstore	chemist
diaper	nappy
hood	bonnet
truck	lorry
duplex apartment	maisonette
apartment	flat
sweater	jumper
flashlight	torch

Preparation—Prior to Departure

A passport is a necessity for international travel. Some countries also require a visa. To obtain a passport, you need proof of U. S. citizenship such as a birth certificate, two identical passport pictures (2x2) and proof of identity. Information available from Foreign Entry Requirements, Consumer Information Center, Pueblo CO 81009, from U. S. passport agencies and most travel agencies. Photocopy your passport in case of loss and carry the copy separately. Contact the American Embassy for passport/visa problems in a foreign country.

Working in a foreign country involves financial and tax changes and these changes should be outlined by your employer. Know how to handle emergencies in the designated country *before you leave this country*. Maps, methods of transportation, and methods of medical assistance should be *prime* considerations. (Note the incident described in Chapter 10, in the section on "International Preparation for Medical Assistance.") Other basic requirements are:

- Knowledge of types of stores that contain goods used daily
- Information on customs, language, weather, driving requirements, types of insurance and local currency.
- Appliance preparation, see information later in this chapter for Appliance Overseas, Incorporated
- Information essential to the running of a household

If you are moving to a country that will require a second language, you will need a working knowledge of the language before you arrive there. In the employee's work situation, there will almost always be an interpreter available, but the person who has to deal with the daily encounters involved in running a household should be able to converse in the language of the country.

Company policies vary as to what employees are allowed to move to a foreign country. Companies usually have some guidelines for the amount, in weight, of furniture, appliances, clothing and dishes that you are permitted to transport. I would advise moving some of your very personal things, such as family pictures and some favorite treasures, to help dispel homesickness. How much you take with you will depend on the amount of time you anticipate for the relocation.

Relocation Agents and Housing

Relocation agents in foreign countries are by far the best friends an unsuspecting expatriate can have. Consider obtaining an agent to assist you in a home purchase and possibly a solicitor's services also. The rules and regulations in buying houses abroad are very different from those governing the purchase of a home in the United States. The clauses and stipulations vary greatly. When you make a decision to relocate, the corporation for whom you work will advise you on the legalities and intricacies of home buying in the country involved.

International Schools

Issues regarding schools (boarding and day), academics, sports and matriculation to other schools are outlined in Chapter 11, Evaluating and Selecting Schools.

Daily Life in a Foreign Country

For a "house spouse" the inconveniences of living abroad can be numerous, so preparations you make before moving will be beneficial. You must be able to find your way around a new country to shop for your goods and be able to locate the ingredients or products you are accustomed to using. I highly recommend purchasing a cookbook published and written especially for the country in which you are residing.

With this book, you will discover the ingredients peculiar to this country and the ingredients will be listed by their proper names, weights and other attributes. If you use cookbooks from the U.S., you must convert your Fahrenheit-gauged recipies to centigrade and change ounces and pounds to milligrams and grams. A kitchen scale becomes indispensable. I finally took the plunge and bought a British cookbook to add to my American collection. It was a very good investment because it simplified dinner preparation considerably.

In a foreign country, day-to-day living, products, foods, names of products, clothes, customs and manners are usually different from those in America. Despite the cultural differences, you can learn and enjoy so much of what another country has to offer. In the beginning many things seem delightfully new and exciting. This can quickly turn into disillusionment after the novelty wears off and it is no longer laughable to try to find your way through the new city or struggle with a strange phone system. As you settle into a routine in the new and different culture, try to adopt the attitude that you are able to learn and enjoy a unique experience. And remember, the situation is temporary, so try to keep things in perspective when challenges arise.

American Women's Organizations

Most countries in Europe have American women's organizations that, aside from being dynamic organizations, serve as a wonderful welcoming committee. These organizations frequently offer a range of fine programs, including art and lecture series, tennis, golf, bridge, travel and antique clubs. These organizations are active in hospitals, Meals on Wheels, and numerous other charitable endeavors. American women's organizations also assist in the acclimation of expatriates by offering them a wealth of information and assistance.

Medical Supplies—Living Abroad

Traveling to a foreign country—and especially residing in one—entails special preparation of medical supplies and personal products. Take note of the following points, and refer to the checklist at the back of the book.

1. Pack an extra supply of prescription medications so that you will not have to have anything refilled until you get settled and acclimated. These medications should be in their own marked containers.

2. Know the correct generic name of medications so a chemist can find an equivalent product.

3. Pack an antidiarrheal medicine.

4. Pack an antibiotic prescribed by your doctor to help contain a severe infection from water or food.

5. Have your prescription for glasses or contact lenses with you. Take enough contact lens solution to last until you find a suitable substitute product. It is advisable to have an extra pair of glasses and/or contact lenses. Eye care products, solutions and contact lenses do vary from country to country.

6. Carry with you the documentation on any medical condition that you or one of your family members has.

7. Be aware of contacts for an English-speaking doctor for the foreign countries you will be visiting or residing in.

> * Note the medical checklist for international travel in the back of the book.

International Association for Medical Assistance for Travelers. This is an excellent contact when planning to travel abroad. Call (716) 754-4883 or write IAMAT at 417 Center Street, Lewiston, NY 14092. Although membership in this nonprofit organization is free, the association gratefully accepts donations to continue their research. An annual directory lists 500 IAMAT centers. These centers are all over the world and can provide you with English- or French-speaking doctors, as well as other benefits.

If you do not speak the language well enough to request pharmacy items, you'll quickly discover that many products, such as feminine napkins, are not displayed. These products ucts are kept behind the counter or in cabinets. To avoid emergencies, pack a two- to three-month supply and when needed take one with you to the chemist to show what you want to purchase. If you are unable to converse in the local language, you may be forced to resort to hand signals, which could be embarrassing or perhaps impossible.

International Dental Information

The following sources will help you obtain a new dentist in a foreign country.

- Dental schools or dental societies
- Dental specialists such as periodontist, endodontist or oral surgeon
- Medical doctor
- Friend or colleague's recommendation.

Appliances in a Foreign Country

Appliances, small and large, deserve special consideration. The outlets, voltage, and wattage are all different. In the United Kingdom, for instance the voltage is 220 compared to 110 in America. This means any appliance taken abroad will require a transformer. These transformers weigh between five and 50 pounds, so they may not be easy to move. Transformers are not recommended for many appliances. If an appliance is used daily, a transformer could shorten that appliance's life span.

A television made for use in one country cannot receive signals in another country. However, it can be used for reviewing material on a videotape. We took our TV and VCR from America to England in order to view special shows or sports activities televised in America. These programs were taped by friends or family in the U.S. and mailed to us. The two units can be attached to a transformer and will then operate satisfactorily.

Electric lights, hairdryers, curling irons and small appliances must all be fitted with special outlet plugs, and some will require a transformer to adjust the voltage and wattage. You must also purchase light bulbs with the correct voltage, so the old light bulbs should be stored until you return. Some appliances, such as a toaster, an iron or a microwave, should be put into storage because they do not work well on a transformer. You can easily purchase one, new or used, in the foreign country. As they move from country to country, fam-

OK HONEY, PLUG IT IN. LET'S SEE IF IT WORKS'

ilies buy and sell all sorts of appliances and furniture through the American women's organizations or through advertisements in local newspapers.

For updated and current information on moving appliances from one country to another, contact **"Appliances Overseas, Incorporated" in New York: (212) 736-7860**. This company suggests making a list of the appliances in your home (noting the wattage of the appliances) that you anticipate moving to another country. Appliances Overseas, Incorporated will supply you with information on the appliances you can move abroad and, if necessary, they will supply step-down transformers to accommodate those you decide to take with you. If you purchase appliances or electrical equipment overseas, contact this company before you return and they will tell you which appliances would be advisable to use in the United States, and which ones should be sold. Many of these may require a step-up transformer.

Homeward Bound

The whole experience of living abroad was considerably more challenging than and different from what my family anticipated, but we grew to love England and the British people. In the years we lived there we came to appreciate a slower paced life-style as well as a significantly older culture.

We count this move as one of the most enriching we ever experienced.

Returning to reside in the United States after a stay abroad is an experience unto itself. Previous moves in and around your own country aren't sufficient preparation for this circumstance. To some extent you can come to think that you have lost that common thread or your "roots." This is an adjustment that many people are not prepared for.

The American Women of Surrey organization in England has a minicourse called "Homeward Bound" for people returning to life in the United States. One of the suggestions this particular program has for a return is to make a change in area and in houses. This tends to give people a different perspective on an old situation.

Moving abroad, my family assumed there would be adjustments to make in another country, but we did not anticipate the many adjustments on reentry to the U.S. Living abroad adds a whole new dimension to your life in so many ways, and returning after several years can make one feel a little out of step, especially if you return to the same city. You cannot move away from an area and just expect to return as though no time has elapsed. Many changes have taken place, not only for yourself but also for the friends you are returning to.

Students who for several years have known the experience of a very culturally mixed classroom, not to mention the international flavor of a foreign school, will experience the same adjustment. Teenagers living abroad with their families typically try to spend their spring breaks in other countries, and participate in sports programs that take them to Paris or Brussels for competition. This is routine for students living and going to school in foreign countries. Therefore, returning to America requires an adjustment, both personally and in the classroom.

Anticipating what to expect and allowing yourself time to adjust will help you to feel in tune in your home country once again. The important thing is to live for the moment, no matter where you reside, and to try to take advantage of whatever each city, state or country has to offer.

21

LEGAL ASPECTS OF MOVING

Estate Laws, Tax Structures and Insurance

Laws, taxes and insurance vary from state to state and sometimes by municipality within each state. Real estate agents can be a good source of this information. You can also obtain information from the local city hall or borough hall on laws, taxes and permits.

Estate laws differ from one state to another and, therefore, you should determine the effect of one state's laws on a will drafted in another state. Any differences could affect the validity of your will. The city, county and state tax structure can also vary considerably. There are many permits to consider, such as occupancy permits, building permits, ordinance permits, moving permits and local government permits. A moving permit is often as little as one dollar, but if you do not have one you may be subject to a fine that would cost considerably more.

Income-management planning and the differences in taxes for your new location can be outlined by an accountant, if you have one. Your age or financial situation may affect the decisions that you make on buying and selling a home. (The following Chapter, Tax Structure—Home Sales, outlined by a certified public accountant, offers more information.)

Insurance policies need to be checked for changes in rates and differentials. These may vary quite a bit from one state to another.

Legal Aspects for International Moves

Relocating to a foreign country requires financial, insurance and accounting changes. International moves are usually corporate moves, primarily due to the fact that working papers are not easily obtained in most countries unless you are a citizen of that country. Your employer should outline the financial aspects in detail for you. Each expatriate's own circumstances will determine how a country's laws and taxes affect them. Some determining factors are your length of stay, resident status, home ownership status and your salary. Income tax advice is available in most American Embassys from U.S. Internal Revenue advisers. Hours vary with time of year.

Local Real Estate Taxes, Zoning and Property Transfer Taxes

by Joseph A. Fitzpatrick, Jr., Attorney at Law with the firm of Fitzpatrick, Lentz & Bubba, Allentown, Pennsylvania.

Local Real Estate Taxes—Before finalizing an agreement for the purchase of a new home, ascertain the assessed valuation of the residential property and the basis on which local governmental units (e.g., town or city, school district, county) establish their tax rates. Reputable real estate firms routinely maintain this type of property tax information and can give a prospective buyer a fairly precise projection of real estate taxes.

Zoning—Before buying a new home, it is advisable to check with the local municipal government to confirm the zoning district in which the new home is located as well as the types of uses which are permitted in that zoning district. It is not uncommon to find municipal zoning ordinances that permit apartments, small businesses and offices in the same district as single-family homes. Also, it is important to determine whether a nonresidential zoning district (e.g., industrial and manufacturing, shopping center-commercial, etc.) adjoins the new home property or is uncomfortably close to the new home property. The location of nonresidential zoning districts near single-family homes can greatly influence the value and resalability of the home as well as the quality of life when adjoining areas develop.

Property Transfer Taxes—Many states have property or "realty transfer" taxes that assess a flat percentage tax on the sale price of any piece of real estate. The total tax may be split between the buyer and seller. The prospective home purchaser should be made aware of any such property transfer taxes, which can represent a very significant part of settlement costs.

22

TAX STRUCTURE
HOME SALES

---

by Luther R. Campbell, Jr., CPA, with the firm of Campbell, Rappold and Yurasits, Allentown, Pennsylvania.

In the year that you sell your home, you must report the sale on your Federal Income Tax Return using Form 2119. On this form you must make one of two decisions:

1. You are not going to replace the home, or you are going to replace the property for less than the net proceeds (selling price less selling costs and home improvement expenses).

2. Within two years you plan to replace the home with more than the net proceeds from the sale.

If your decision is covered by item #1, you pay the tax as determined by the gain and the matter is closed.

If your decision is covered by item #2, you can elect to defer the payment of the tax by rolling over the gain into the new home. If the purchase of the new home occurs during the same tax year, you will complete Form 2119 by reflecting the purchase and rollover. If the purchase of the new home occurs after the tax year of the sale, you have two years to file an amended tax return for the year of the sale. In this case you must complete Form 2119, reflecting this purchase and establishing the beginning tax basis of the new home. If for any reason you did not replace the property (1) within the two-year deferrment, or (2) within the year purchased, or (3) you bought a less expensive home than the net proceeds, then the tax plus interest must be paid back to the filing date of the year of sale return.

If you have doubts regarding the purchase of a new residence, and you wish to avoid the payment of interest, you can elect to pay the tax in the year of sale and later within the two year period. If the property is replaced, you can file an amended return for the year of sale and get a refund.

If, however, you are 55 years of age or older and have used the home as your primary residence for three of the past five years, you can claim a one time only exemption of $125,000 to the federal government. For example, the tax structure equals: Sale price of home, less recent closing costs, less original purchase price and closing costs, less home improvements. Exclude the first $125,000 and pay capital gains on the remaining amount. In addition, you have the individual state taxes to contend with, which will vary.

23

RETIREMENT RELOCATION

Geographic Location

As you approach retirement, there are many reasons why you may consider a geographical move. Relocating from a cold to a warm climate is just one of the reasons. This would mean no snow to shovel, no ice to slip on and less need for heavy garments (less clothing variety will mean less expense). The cold versus warm debate may not even enter into your decision; you may just feel the need to relocate for any one of a number of reasons. Retirees often consider relocating to a smaller home with less maintenance, upkeep and (possibly) lower taxes.

Whatever the reason you are considering a geographic change, it should be well-thought-out (preferably years in advance) and then taken slowly. Spend at least one year—and preferably two—to complete a permanent retirement change. It would be dreadful to make an emotional move, sell your house and relocate only to find that you absolutely hate the situation or the area.

If you have been vacationing in an area, and therefore know it well, you are better prepared when considering a move. Even so, vacationing and residing permanently in an area are two very different experiences.

In choosing a future retirement community you have not only the climate to consider but also the number of retirees such as yourself. Is this a community in which you will feel comfortable on a long-term basis? Is this a thriving community? What activities are available? Church, theater, sports, recreational facilities, and all the things that you enjoy doing now: Are they available in the area you are considering?

The Transition From Work to Retirement

When you retire, you may consider working part-time or devoting some time to a charitable organization. Consultation work or a small amount of the work of your trade will ease the transition and bring in some income too.

Having worked regular hours for many years, retirees find that it is important to have some routine to the day. Set aside a certain time in each day for chores, a part-time job and, most importantly, exercise. You may feel as though you want to enjoy the "good life" and loaf in the sun, but this can be quite a drastic change, and one that can very quickly become unsettling.

Charity work can be a valuable and gratifying way to help those in need in your community. You need only check with local churches or your newspaper to learn of a few areas where volunteers can help.

Career Change

Retirement may be the most drastic career change that you have ever made and thus it should be given respect and consideration. Make lists of needs and wants for yourself, your home and your area. Your annual income will most likely change after retirement, so you must consider your cash outlay carefully. It is important to retire into a home and a community that you can afford financially and enjoy to the fullest.

Things to Consider When Relocating

1. Your basic skills
2. Your hobbies
3. Recreational activities
4. Medical facilities—if you or your spouse becomes incapacitated, what medical facilities are available? Nursing homes?
5. Life-style of the area you are considering
6. Local laws, *estate taxes*: how would these taxes affect you or your family—check with your lawyer and accountant
7. Percentage of retirees in the community
8. The house you purchase— appropriate for you presently as well as if someone becomes incapacitated
9. The house you purchase—in a good resale location, with a good school system
10. Note the chapter on selling a home when you are over 55 years of age, entitled "Tax Structure - Home Sales"
11. Community services that may welcome volunteers

EPILOGUE

Expectation Versus Realization

Moving requires the utmost cooperation and organization. It must be a united family effort. Moving can and should be a chance to expand horizons and learn more about different cities, states, countries, people and cultures, but you must do it together. Because of my family's moves and travels, we have developed friendships with people all over the United States as well as in England, Ireland, France, Spain, Malaysia, Tokyo and Singapore. We consider ourselves richer for the experiences.

Our children had difficulty adjusting at times, as we all did, but we believe we are stronger as individuals and as a family because of the challenges we encountered. To be sure, our children were all triumphant academically and socially and we commend them. Without their help and cooperation, we could not have accomplished all that we did as a family.

Changing residences and schools is not a prospect to be taken lightly. Relocations must be treated with forethought; the people in them, with care and love. In this way, the new situation can ultimately become a positive encounter.

All of us are a sum total of our heritage and our experiences. Anytime you have the opportunity to enjoy another culture, a distant area or a distant land, you should do so with solid preparation and ample zest. As a friend who has experienced several moves and at one time administered employee moves for a major corporation expressed it, "Moving is neither good nor bad, it is only thinking that makes it so."

The gap between the expectation and the realization in any endeavor is what creates a good (or bad) life experience. When our expectations are high and we expect a move to proceed like clockwork, but the move proves to be a disaster—that is realization. We can have some control over this expectation-realization clash. The purpose of this book is to give you the tools to organize a move and to make it successful. If you are *amply prepared* for a relocation, the expectation and realization should be more one and the same.

As my friends in England all liked to say, "I wish you all the best."

CHECKLISTS

*For your convenience, the author gladly gives
permission to photocopy these checklists.*

ADDRESS CHANGES

Make a complete list of these items, note dates of changes on each item and *keep this list*. Update or change as necessary.

Send cards with your new address to relatives and friends.

	Date Notified	Date Effective
Driver's license	_____	_____
Car registration	_____	_____
Voter registration	_____	_____
Magazines and periodicals	_____	_____
allow 6 weeks to change	_____	_____
(use address label on the	_____	_____
magazine to expedite the	_____	_____
change)	_____	_____
	_____	_____
	_____	_____
Credit cards	_____	_____
	_____	_____
Charge accounts	_____	_____
	_____	_____
	_____	_____
Insurance company	_____	_____
Investments	_____	_____
Stockbroker	_____	_____
College bursar's offices	_____	_____
Finance companies/car loan	_____	_____
Bank	_____	_____
Airline frequent flier cards	_____	_____
Others	_____	_____
	_____	_____
	_____	_____
	_____	_____

CONTACTS FOR FINAL BIllING

	Date Notified	Date Effective
Telephone company	_____	_____
Long-distance telephone company	_____	_____
Electric company	_____	_____
Gas company	_____	_____
Oil service	_____	_____
Dry cleaner	_____	_____
Diaper service	_____	_____
Newspaper	_____	_____
Tax collector	_____	_____
Trash collector	_____	_____
Television cable	_____	_____
Lawn service	_____	_____
Any other services	_____	_____
	_____	_____
	_____	_____

Necessary Items to Take With You

1. House keys for the new home _____
2. Spare keys for your car _____
3. Address book with telephone numbers of family and friends _____
4. Telephone directory (from city you are leaving) _____
5. Cooking utensils (a small supply) _____
6. Pet identification tag with new address, if you have it _____
7. Children's games or something to occupy them for the trip _____
8. Snacks and drinks for family _____

Include the following items too. Note separate checklist for each.

9. Survival box—contents very important _____
10. Pet supplies _____
11. Address-change list _____
12. File of pertinent records _____

FILE FOR PERTINENT RECORDS

1. Documents from the moving company (refering to documents itemizing your complete move so you have a record of your household items) _____

   *Have a contact for the moving company in the new city _____

   *Moving company should have a contact for you in the new city _____

2. Medical records _____

3. Dental records (include dental specialists) _____

4. Pharmacy records for family _____

5. Prescriptions for necessary medications _____

6. List of recommended or referred doctors _____

7. School records for your students _____

8. List of current academic subjects and books or readers _____

9. Birth certificates for students beginning school _____

10. Inoculation records for child for school _____

11. Household inventory _____

12. Insurance files _____

    Personal _____

    Auto _____

    Medical _____

13. Legal documents and bankbook _____

14. Pet records _____

15. Map of new city _____

The documents that you take on your travel depend on your individual circumstances, the time of year and how long your household goods will be unavailable to you. For instance, if your belongings will be in storage for 10 months while a house is being built, you will need more records than if you were making a direct move from one house to another.

SURVIVAL BOX

Items to have on hand for your departure moving day and the day you move into your new home.

Paper/scratch pad/stamps/envelopes   _____

Pen/pencil/marking pens   _____

Cellophane tape/heavy-duty tape   _____

Scissors/pocketknife   _____

Tape measure/collapsible ruler   _____

Paper cups—hot and cold-bags with zipper closure   _____

Paper plates/napkins/disposable utensils   _____

Instant coffee/tea/powdered creamer/sugar   _____

Paper towels/facial tissue/toilet tissue   _____

Soap/disposable towelettes   _____

Aspirin/adhesive bandages   _____

Gallon bottle of drinking water   _____

Can opener/bottle opener/corkscrew   _____

Travel alarm   _____

Flashlight   _____

Small tool kit   _____

An ice chest for beverages, medicine or anything that requires refrigeration   _____

PET SUPPLIES FOR DOMESTIC TRAVEL

Water _____

Food _____

Leash _____

Toy _____

Identification tag with new address, if possible _____

Article of clothing from a family member for pet to to lie on, or something the pet is used to for comfort (Pets can get confused and become a problem, especially if they are not used to travel. Avoid unnecessary difficulties during your move.) _____

Kennel for travel _____

Veterinarian papers with all medical records Possible sedative, on veterinarian's advice (Know how your animal will tolerate travel.) *Shots should be up-to-date, rabies especially* _____

PET SUPPLIES FOR INTERNATIONAL TRAVEL

Make airline travel arrangements *early* _____

Water _____

Enough food for pet to last until you find a brand in your new location that agrees with your pet (Give no food during the trip) _____

Leash _____

Toy _____

Identification tag with new address, if possible _____

Article of clothing, see Article above _____

Kennel—size very important for this trip. Pet should be able to stand up, turn around and lie down in natural positions _____

Veterinarian records
There will be regulations to follow for this move. Check with the airlines or a good U.S. kennel for the latest information.
*See Veterinarian above _____

SELLING A HOME

Preparing Your Home For The Best Appearance

The outside: the first thing a buyer will see.

Trim and fertilize lawns, shrubs and trees. _____

Clear debris from lawn or around the border of home. _____

Plant flowers, depending on the season of the year, to give a cheery appearance. _____

Paint and clean the front door. _____

Make sure garage door is working properly. _____

Keep paths and patios in good repair. _____

Keep outside paint fresh—no chipping or peeling. _____

Clean and paint windows—make sure they fit well. _____

Attach and paint shutters. _____

Paint mailbox and flower boxes. _____

Make sure house numbers are visible. _____

SELLING A HOME

Preparing Your Home For The Best Appearance

The inside: initial impression may make the sale.

Maintain a fresh environment (no animal odors or any other odors). _____

Keep house clean and tidy. _____

Put fresh towels in bathrooms. _____

Clean windows. _____

Clean walls and woodwork—no marks or fingerprints. _____

Keep counters as clear as possible (not too many appliances in view). _____

Clean all appliances that remain with the house and provide appropriate literature for these appliances. _____

Straighten closets—people open doors to check sizes _____

Make sure hinges and knobs are tightened. _____

Fix any leaky faucets. _____

Have as few people and animals around as possible when the house is shown. _____

Keep your home ready to be shown at all times, in case of short notice from real estate agent. _____

Home Shopping

Key Points to Consider

Price of home—realistic? comparison of prices in area?   _____

Homes sold in the area? How recent? Price?   _____

Age of the home?   _____

Taxes on the home?   _____

Repairs or renovations necessary?   _____

Floor plan—square footage of home and lot   _____

   Will rooms accommodate your furniture?   _____

   Room to expand, if necessary?   _____

Bedrooms—amount & closet space   _____

Bathrooms—amount, size & accessibility   _____

Extra rooms—type and special features   _____

Landscaping—maintenance or improvements necessary?   _____

Dining room size _____ Kitchen size   _____

Colors of rooms—necessary to change?   _____

Security system/fire alarm & smoke detectors?   _____

Garage door automatic opener?   _____

Heating system—brand, monthly costs   _____

Air conditioner—brand, monthly costs   _____

Utilities and costs   _____

Appliances—age and brand   _____

   In good repair or dealer accessible?   _____

HOME SHOPPING

Key Points to Consider

Wiring and insulation, adequate now & future? ———————

Noise level—highways, now or future? ———————

  airport nearby? ———————

Area of the home, good for resale? ———————

Check distances to the following:

  Work ———————

  Schools ———————

  Churches ———————

  Doctors ———————

  Hospitals ———————

  Playgrounds ———————

  Airport ———————

  Shopping ———————

Zoning laws of the area, could they be changed? ———————

Consider these points also when you are shopping homes and areas.

Monthly income available for mortgage payments ———————

Available money for utilities/maintenance/
  repair of appliances or
  any other equipment in the home ———————

Available money for improvements: paint/paper/
  drapes/carpets ———————

MEDICAL AND DENTAL
DOMESTIC TRAVEL

1. Take extra prescription medications (noting shelf life of medicines).
   Bring enough medicines to last until you get acclimated to your
   new area.

2. Keep all drugs in their *own containers* that are labeled appropriately with the *name of the drug, the strength and the dosage.*

3. Know how medications should be stored. Some should not be
   kept in the bathroom due to the humidity changes.

4. Know the side effects of medications and if any food or beverages should be avoided while taking a medication.

5. Know whether driving should be avoided while taking a particular drug.

6. Take a copy of your phamacist's file on your family.

7. Note specific medical conditions that you or your family have.
   Carry the clarification and documentation with you to your new
   destination.

8. Inquire about a specialist *before moving* to the new city if a
   member of your family has a condition that warrants this kind
   of medical care.

Note sources of information on finding a new doctor and a new dentist
in Chapter 10, Selecting Quality Medical and Dental Care.

MEDICAL AND DENTAL
INTERNATIONAL TRAVEL

All of the points listed on the previous page for travel in the United States will apply to international travel. Also note the following:

1. Regulations on medicines vary from country to country. Some drugs that are sold over the counter in foreign countries may not be sold or used in the United States without a prescription. Some drugs may even be illegal in the U.S. If you should acquire any pills or solutions while traveling abroad, it would be advisable to check with your doctor or pharmacist on drug regulations.

2. Pharmacists can supply the correct generic name of any medicines you are taking to ensure acquiring an equivalent product in another country. Many medicines are the same from country to country; however, the trade name of a drug may vary.

3. Antidiarrheal medicine should be included when traveling abroad.

4. Antibiotics prescribed by your doctor can be taken abroad if you are prone to severe infections.

5. Eye care
   a. Carry a copy of your prescription for eyeglasses or contact lenses with you.
   b. Take along an extra pair of eyeglasses or contact lenses.
   c. Products and solutions for contact lenses vary from country to country, so take along extra products to use until you find a suitable equivalent.

Note sources of information on finding a new doctor and a new dentist in Chapter 10, Selecting Quality Medical and Dental Care.

FINAL WEEK

Last Minute Details

Things to do before you leave your old residence.

Organize individual rooms. _____

Mark items for moving, storage or "Do Not Pack." _____

Take *anything* out of these rooms that you will need
for your trip or will want to take with you. _____

Return all library books. _____

Pick up clothing at the cleaners. _____

Prepare your appliances for moving:
oven/stove/washer/dryer
refrigerator (empty and defrost)
  Check appliance manuals for this information.
  See also page 67 for guidelines _____

Empty your safe-deposit box at the bank. _____

Set aside your vacuum cleaner and cleaning supplies. _____

Contact all services and utilities for final date of
service and billing information. _____

Take pictures of furniture and other items that you
will want to reference (for color) before your
goods are delivered to your home. _____

Check with post office personnel to make sure they
have your forwarding address as well as your departure and arrival dates. _____

Check your survival box—make sure it's complete. _____

Check your file folder for all your records. _____

DEPARTURE DAY

Before departing your home—Take one last walk through the entire house and check the following areas. Make sure everything in the house that should be packed, has been!

Check: closets   _____

       shelves   _____

       drawers to permanent cabinets   _____

       storage areas   _____

       basement   _____

       garage   _____

Clean and vacuum house. _____

Check heat temperature in the house; set appropriately. _____

Make sure all lights are turned off. _____

Appliances should be turned off—check oven. _____

Windows should be closed and locked. _____

Doors should be closed and locked. _____

Leave a forwarding address and telephone number for yourself with a neighbor, in case of problems. _____

Give a reliable friend or neighbor a key if your home is not sold. _____

Lock the house. _____

*Note—if you are moving before you have sold your home:

Notify the police and your insurance agent that the house is vacant.

Borrow some old lamps from a neighbor and set them in the house on electric timers. Give this neighbor a key to your home.

Make sure the lawn is cut and maintained, or snow is shoveled, whatever is appropriate.

It is important that the house is cared for so it is not obviously vacant. Unfortunately, vandalism can occur with empty houses, so take precautions.

MOVING YOURSELF
EQUIPMENT NEEDED

Anticipation of a move should inspire you to *save and collect* wrapping paper and boxes from any sources you can! Materials from deliveries arriving to your home or purchases you make are two examples. You'll find many sources of free and useful packing material.

Start collecting sturdy boxes. Liquor store boxes are especially good due to their partitions. (Used boxes of many kinds can be purchased from moving companies.) _____

Save cardboard, bubble paper, tissue paper. _____

Save or buy paper for wrapping (no newspaper); newspaper is good for padding only. _____

Buy ample cording or rope, which is necessary to secure furniture in the truck about every quarter of the truck capacity. _____

Purchase sturdy tape/marking pens/labels. _____

Set aside old blankets or padding. _____

Obtain a substantial lock to use on the rear of the truck. _____

Many supplies can be purchased from self-help or other moving companies, but save whatever you can to keep your expenses down.

MOVING YOURSELF
PREPARATIONS TO MAKE

Make a household inventory.
This is necessary for insurance claims and it makes the job of estimating the amount of boxes you will need easier.   _____

Check *survival box list* for items to have on hand.   _____

Pack any items not being used, as early as possible.   _____

Pick up a pamphlet for information on moving yourself. Many self-help companies have booklets, which are free. Ryder's *Mover's Advantage* is comprehensive, informative and easy to use.   _____

Reserve a truck at least one month in advance (earlier, if it is peak moving time).   _____

Reserve your equipment/dollies/blankets or pads.   _____

Check on your personal insurance policy, plus the truck rental company's insurance, to ensure adequate coverage for yourself, your helpers and your household effects.   _____

Engage some dependable help and ask them to *reserve* the moving dates.   _____

CHECKLIST FOR NEW CITY

1. Locate new doctors' and dentists' offices. _____

2. Locate the nearest hospital. _____

3. Open a bank account and reserve a safe-deposit box in a bank branch convenient to your new home. _____

4. Take your students to their new school, introduce them to any teachers available. _____

5. Locate school bus stops for children. _____

6. Acquire a city map, if you do not have one. Proceed to acquaint yourself with the new city, noting hospitals, pharmacies, churches, restaurants, markets, dry cleaners, beauty shops, barbers and other services used by your family. _____

7. Visit your chamber of commerce to become aware of activities and functions in your new city. _____

8. Register to vote. _____

9. Subscribe to a newspaper. _____

*Note: Consider sending some flowers to the house spouse who is organizing the move.

CHECKLIST FOR NEW CITY

10. Secure a local telephone directory. _____

11. Send for an identification tag for your pet with your new address. _____

12. Check newspaper for handymen and local services. Real estate agents can be of help with some of the handymen, and they often know of painters and paperhangers too. _____

13. Arrange for service to begin in your home for:

    electrical _____

    telephone _____

    gas _____

    water _____

    trash collection _____

    television cable _____

14. Check with your local post office personnel to be sure they know you are moving into the area. Give them your new and old addresses. Note * below. _____

* If you are in a temporary area for several weeks, you can sign a form at the post office to have your mail held there for you. This will mean trips to the post office, but it is easier than two address changes.

INDEX

Furniture, 23-25
  measuring and drawing to scale,
    23, 24
  unusually large pieces, 24

G

Garage sale, 15-17
  marking system, 16
  pricing, 16
  advertisement, 17
Geographic location. *See* Retirement relocation
Goals in buying a house. *See*
  Home

H

Help, moving. *See* Moving
Home
  building as an option, 21
  buying, 19
  capital gains (after Age 55), 91
  down payment, buying with-
    out, 40
  environmental issues, 28
  goals in buying, 27
  negotiating a transaction to buy,
    40
  older, buying and potential
    problems, 20
  pictures and floor plan, 29
  prices to sell, 11
  renting, reasons for, 22
  selecting an area, 28
  selling tips, 11-13
  settlement day, 13, 35
  shopping, 27
Houseplants, during a move, 76

I

Improvements for investment.
  See Building a home
Insurance for moving oneself. *See*
  Moving
International Association for
  Medical Assistance for Travel-
  ers, 46, 85
International relocation, 81-88
  appliances in a foreign country,
    86, 87

daily life in a foreign country,
  83
dental assistance, 46, 86
medical assistance, 46, 85
medical supplies, 84. *See also*
  Checklists
preparation (prior to departure), 82
relocation agents, 83
schools. *See* Schools
Inventory, household goods, 6

L

Legal aspects of moving, 89, 90

M

Measuring furniture. *See* Furniture
Medical, international travel, 84
  See also Checklists
  international preparation, 44
  medical supplies, 84
  source of information on find-
    ing a new dentist, 86
  sources of information on find-
    ing a new doctor, 85
Medical, domestic moves, 43. *See
  also* Checklists
  prescriptions/pharmacy   re-
    cords, 44
  questions to ask for a new doc-
    tor, 44
  records, preparing for a move,
    43
  sources of information on find-
    ing a new dentist, 46
  sources of information on find-
    ing a new doctor, 45, 46
Mortgage rates, 38
  prequalifying and preapproval,
    39
  types of, 38
Moving, to new house with a
  moving company, 69
  documents, signing of, 71
  orienting the movers, 69, 70
Moving yourself, 73
  appliance preparation, 67, 75

equipment needed, 73
help, organizing, 74
insurance required, 76
loading the truck, 75
packing, 75
rules of the company, 76

N

Negotiating a homes sales transaction, 40
New city, adjusting in, 77
suggestions to make yourself at home, 79

O

Older home, building, buying, problems. See Home
Options, buy, build or rent, 19-22
Organizing rooms. See Rooms

P

Painting, neutral colors in homes sales, 12
Prescriptions/pharmacy records. See Medical
Pictures of home, 29
Price, realistic (selling a home), 11

R

Real estate agent, criteria to select, 37
Retirement relocation, 93
career change, 95
geographic location/change, 93
things to consider in relocating, 95
transition, 94
Room plots
drawing, 25
posting for moves, 69
Rooms, organizing, 65
Rules of the moving company, 76

S

Schools, evaluating and selecting, 47-50
boarding, international, 50
criteria to select, 47
international school systems, 49
school considerations, before relocating, 49
types of international schools, 49
U.S. Department of Education, information and guidelines on schools, 48
School, problems. See Children
Selling a home. See Home
Services, household, termination, 12
Settlement day,
building a home, 35
selling a home, 13
Survival box, for moving day, 8
See also Checklists
Survival box, children, 9

T

Tax structure, 91, 92
Taxes
local real estate, 90
property transfer, 90
Telephone contacts, 8
Template, 25
Transition, work to retirement, 94

U

Utility companies and services, contact for billing, 6

W

Work force in the nineties, 1

Z

Zoning, 90

Notes

Notes

About the Author

Beverly Roman was thrust into the moving scene very early in her career after receiving an R.N. degree and making her first move to a location 1,000 miles from home. This was one of six moves while single, followed by 16 additional moves after marriage to a naval officer in 1961. The family "moving career" began with the United States Navy, followed by others when her husband joined a Fortune 500 company in 1967.

The author is experienced in organizing the family's personal moves within the United States, as well as a move to Europe. She also spent several years guiding grade school students to successfully improve their study habits and school grades.

A book of this type was suggested to the author numerous times by friends who were not only astonished by the number of moves the family made, but the success with which it was managed. Happily, the family unit is still intact and thriving. In fact, the Romans' have three grown children who have moved several times on their own and say that they benefited from the tips outlined in this book.

About the Illustrator

Michael J. Cadieux was born in Wichita Falls, Texas, in 1967. Michael traveled and lived in many states due to his father's career in the United States Air Force. Michael currently resides in Gainsville, Florida, where he recently graduated from the University of Florida with a Bachelor of Design degree. Michael has been involved in the art department of a local Florida television station. This book contains his first published illustrations.